# 跟我学汉语
# Chinese with Me

## 汉字课本(二)
## A Chinese Character Course Book (II)

沈 玮 编著

图书在版编目(CIP)数据

跟我学汉语·汉字课本(二)/沈玮编著. —北京：北京大学出版社，2012.8
（北大版对外汉语教材·短期培训系列）
ISBN 978-7-301-21112-0

Ⅰ.跟… Ⅱ.沈… Ⅲ.汉语–对外汉语教学–教材 Ⅳ.H195.4

中国版本图书馆CIP数据核字(2012)第189532号

| | |
|---|---|
| 书　　　　名： | 跟我学汉语·汉字课本（二） |
| 著作责任者： | 沈　玮　编著 |
| 责 任 编 辑： | 李　凌 |
| 标 准 书 号： | ISBN 978-7-301-21112-0/H·3113 |
| 出 版 发 行： | 北京大学出版社 |
| 地　　　　址： | 北京市海淀区成府路205号　100871 |
| 网　　　　址： | http://www.pup.cn |
| 电　　　　话： | 邮购部 62752015　发行部 62750672　编辑部 62753374　出版部 62754962 |
| 电 子 邮 箱： | zpup@pup.pku.edu.cn |
| 印　刷　者： | 北京大学印刷厂 |
| 经　销　者： | 新华书店 |
| | 880毫米×1230毫米　大16开本　11.5印张　251千字 |
| | 2012年8月第1版　2019年5月第3次印刷 |
| 定　　　　价： | 34.00元（含光盘一张） |

未经许可，不得以任何方式复制或抄袭本书之部分或全部内容。
**版权所有，侵权必究**　**举报电话**：010-62752024
　　　　　　　　　　　　**电子邮箱**：fd@pup.pku.edu.cn

# 使用说明

**概述**

《跟我学汉语·汉字课本》(二)是《跟我学汉语·综合课本》(二)的系列配套教材之一,它选取了出现在《综合课本》并且是留学生日常生活中经常接触的407个汉字和部首(其中汉字399个,不成字的部首8个,复习第一册的部首不计入)。编排时以部首为主线,通过部首引出生字;以声旁为副线,通过同声旁汉字比较横向串联所学汉字,并通过声旁加新部首扩展汉字量。《跟我学汉语·汉字课本》在正式出版前经过了长达五年的课堂使用和修改,被证明是非常符合非汉字文化圈学生认知特点的汉字入门教材。

**汉字来源及与《综合课本》的关系**

《汉字课本》(二)承接《汉字课本》(一),并与《综合课本》(二)的15个单元相对应,从16单元至30单元。如《汉字课本》(二)第18单元所教的汉字来自《综合课本》第18单元课文和第18单元前课文中的汉字,而且汉字阅读练习中编写的词汇和句子也和《综合课本》第18单元的课文内容基本呼应。因此,《汉字课本》和《综合课本》配套使用,教学效果更佳。学完《汉字课本》(一)第1—15单元后,可以用2—4课时分别学习《汉字课本》(二)的第16—30单元。当然,《汉字课本》的编排体系很完整,也可以单独作为汉字入门教材使用。

**内容、形式及教学方法**

《汉字课本》(二)注意与《汉字课本》(一)的衔接和所学汉字的复现。开始部分是一张完整的汉字笔画名称表,便于学生复习。主体部分每单元由以下四大部分组成:

一、旧部首和新汉字。

这部分先复习《汉字课本》(一)第1—15单元学过的若干个部首,给出部首的通用中文名称和英文意思。同时学习带有这些部首的新汉字,并给出它们常用的英文意思和若干常用中文词组(绝大多数词组由所学过的汉字组成,没有学过的汉字加注了拼音)。对某些汉字的字形或字义还进行了灵活的分析,有些解释可能并非该汉字的本义,目的在于帮助学生识记。

此外,还设计了针对这部分内容的一些小练习。其中的阅读扩展练习,从词语开始逐步扩展,最终成为句子,以此提高汉字的复现率,通过集中操练帮助学生认读,同时也能训练学生的汉语构句能力。涉及的语法点和句型均已在《跟我学汉语·综合课本》对应的课文中学过。这部分练习内容教师可以让学生在课堂上阅读,时间不够也可以让学生在课后准备,下次课堂上检查。书后附有该部分句子的参考译文。没有学过的汉字标注了拼音。

二、新部首和新汉字。

这部分介绍了若干个新部首(包括其单独成字的形式和作为部首的形式)及带有该部首的新汉字,还包含了一些独体字或没有归入部首的字。体例与第一部分基本相同。

三、新声旁及汉字扩展。

这部分针对汉字形声字多的特点,介绍新的常用声旁及带有该声旁的若干汉字,培养学生汉字扩展的学能。该部分后面的练习希望学生通过自学加深对形声字规律的理解。

四、综合练习。

这部分设计了数量丰富、形式多样的练习,可供教师在课堂上做巩固练习或者学生课后个别复习使用,教师可根据课时灵活安排。

其中的阅读练习,对应《跟我学汉语·综合课本》(二)课文的第二段,已学过的汉字不再标注拼音。

写汉字练习展示了本单元所学全部汉字的笔顺,并让学生练习书写。

书后附有全书练习参考答案、参考译文、每单元所教汉字和汉字音序索引。

另外,本书还附光盘一张,主要内容是本教材汉字和部首的幻灯片,以便学习生字、打印字卡。

沈玮

2011年12月

# Contents

## 目 录

| | |
|---|---|
| Review | 1 |
| Unit 16　人(亻)、女、寸、彳、主 | 3 |
| Unit 17　冫、氵、气、穴、雨、隹、分 | 13 |
| Unit 18　囗、火(灬)、户、疒、足(𧾷)、方 | 23 |
| Unit 19　辶、广、力、止、舟、巴 | 33 |
| Unit 20　车、走、田、又、夂、正 | 43 |
| Unit 21　心(忄)、金(钅)、刀(刂)、目、里、肖 | 53 |
| Unit 22　言(讠)、耳、戈、立、竹(⺮)、争 | 64 |
| Unit 23　手(扌)、攵、页、旦 | 75 |
| Unit 24　禾、欠、方、巾、羊 | 85 |
| Unit 25　门、丝(纟)、邑(阝)、示(礻)、包 | 94 |
| Unit 26　囗、宀、草(艹)、衣(衤)、风 | 105 |
| Unit 27　厂、月、刂、玉(王)、专 | 115 |
| Unit 28　土、贝、石、马 | 125 |
| Unit 29　食(饣)、日、阜(阝)、山、夕、青 | 135 |
| Unit 30　木、丶、匚、冂、亠、交 | 146 |
| Appendix 1　Keys to Exercises　练习参考答案 | 156 |
| Appendix 2　Translations for Reference　参考译文 | 159 |
| Appendix 3　Characters Taught in Each Unit　每单元所教汉字 | 167 |
| Appendix 4　Index of Characters　汉字音序索引 | 171 |

# Review 复习

# Name of the strokes
# 汉字笔画名称表

| Number | Chinese stokes (笔画) | Name (名称) | Example characters (例字) |
|---|---|---|---|
| 1 | 一 | 横 héng | 大 |
| 2 | 一フ | 横折 héng zhé | 口 |
| 3 | フ | 横撇 héng piě | 水 |
| 4 | ㄱ | 横钩 héng gōu | 你 |
| 5 | 丁 | 横折钩 héng zhé gōu | 月 |
| 6 | 了 | 横撇弯钩 héng piě wān gōu | 阳 |
| 7 | ㄥ | 横折提 héng zhé tí | 课 |
| 8 | ㄥ | 横折弯 héng zhé wān | 没 |
| 9 | ㄟ | 横折弯钩 héng zhé wān gōu | 九 |
| 10 | 弓 | 横折折折钩 héng zhé zhé zhé gōu | 汤 |
| 11 | ㄟ | 横斜钩 héng xié gōu | 风 |
| 12 | 孑 | 横折折撇 héng zhé zhé piě | 及 |
| 13 | ㄴ | 横折折 héng zhé zhé | 凹 |
| 14 | 弓 | 横折折折 héng zhé zhé zhé | 凸 |
| 15 | 丨 | 竖 shù | 十 |

1

| Number | Chinese stokes (笔画) | Name (名称) | Example characters (例字) |
|---|---|---|---|
| 16 | 亅 | 竖钩 shù gōu | 小 |
| 17 | 乚 | 竖弯钩 shù wān gōu | 元 |
| 18 | ↓ | 竖提 shù tí | 食 |
| 19 | ㄴ | 竖折 shù zhé | 山 |
| 20 | 𠃌 | 竖折折钩 shù zhé zhé gōu | 吗 |
| 21 | ㄴ | 竖弯 shù wān | 四 |
| 22 | ㄣ | 竖折撇 shù zhé piě | 专 |
| 23 | ㇉ | 竖折折 shù zhé zhé | 鼎 |
| 24 | 丿 | 撇 piě | 八 |
| 25 | ㄥ | 撇折 piě zhé | 去 |
| 26 | ㄑ | 撇点 piě diǎn | 女 |
| 27 | 丶 | 点 diǎn | 广 |
| 28 | ㇏ | 捺 nà | 人 |
| 29 | ノ | 提 tí | 地 |
| 30 | ㇂ | 斜钩 xié gōu | 我 |
| 31 | 亅 | 弯钩 wān gōu | 了 |
| 32 | ㇌ | 卧钩 wò gōu | 心 |

**练习**

请写出含有以上笔画的汉字各两个。

# Unit 16

## I Old radicals and new characters
### 旧部首和新汉字

rén
人（亻）
rén zì tóu　dān rénpáng
人字头（单人旁）
person

- 会：人+云 ▶ to meet, meeting; can
  (huì) (yún)
  * when people have a meeting, they will gather together like clouds
  开会　大会

- 位：亻+立 ▶ location
  (wèi) (lì)
  * the place where a person stands is the location
  座位　一位

- 信：亻+言 ▶ letter; to believe
  (xìn) (yán)
  * a letter is to write down the words a person wants to say or to believe what people said
  写信　相信
  (xiě)

- 全：人+王 ▶ whole
  (quán) (wáng)
  * the king has everything he wants
  全家　全国

- 化：亻+匕 ▶ to change
  (huà) (bǐ)
  * a person holds a knife to change the form of something
  文化　化学

- 件：亻+牛 ▶ measure word
  (jiàn) (niú)
  两件　文件

3

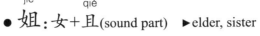

- 姐 (jiě)：女＋且 (qiě)(sound part) ▶elder, sister

  *"女" is the radical for girl or woman, "且" is a picture of a stool(冂) with two rungs(二) standing on the ground(一), the character shows a lady is sitting on a stool and making up

  姐姐　姐妹 (mèi)

- 如 (rú)：女＋口 (kǒu) ▶as if

  * a woman does things according to the words someone said

  如果　比如

- 始 (shǐ)：女＋台 (tái) ▶to begin

  * nose(厶) and mouth(口) stand for a head which is a begin of a body

  开始　起始

- 要 (yào)：西＋女 (xī) ▶to want, to need

  * women always want something

  不要　只要

## Exercises 1（练习一）

**1. Choose the correct characters（选择正确的汉字）:**

（1）can　　　　A. 全　　B. 会
（2）if　　　　　A. 如　　B. 始
（3）letter　　　A. 认　　B. 信
（4）position　　A. 化　　B. 位
（5）to want　　 A. 西　　B. 要

**2. Reading（读一读，认汉字）:**

开会　开大会　公司开大会　下午公司开大会。　下午公司开大会吗？

几位　几位客人　有几位客人　饭店里有几位客人？

相信　不相信　相信不相信　我们相信他。　你们相信不相信他？

全家　全家在家　星期天全家在家　星期天全家在家吃午饭。

文化　中国文化　学中国文化　想学中国文化　我想学中国文化。

姐姐　一个姐姐　有一个姐姐　她有一个姐姐。　她有一个姐姐,我没有姐姐。

如果　如果下雨　如果下雨我不来。　如果不下雨　如果不下雨我来。

开始　什么时候开始　什么时候开始学习　什么时候开始学习汉语?

要　不要　要不要　不要给他打电话　我要不要给他打电话?

## II New radicals and characters
### 新部首和新汉字

<table>
<tr><td>

cùn
寸
cùn zì páng
寸字旁
a person's pulse on the wrist

</td><td>

● 寸(cùn): a unit of length equal to one-third decimeter; very small

\* 一寸,寸土

● 对(duì): 又+寸　▶right; vs; opposite

\* both parts are related to hand, palm to palm

不对　对手

● 导(dǎo): 巳(sì)+寸　▶to lead

\* the upper part "巳" likes winding road, and the down part "寸" stands for hand, using hand to lead the direction

辅(fǔ)导　导游(yóu)

</td></tr>
</table>

<table>
<tr><td>

chì
彳
shuāngrénpáng
双人旁
walk slowly

</td><td>

● 很(hěn): 彳+艮(gèn)(sound part)　▶very

\* the right part "艮" is not only a sound part but also a meaning part, it originally means limitation, so "很" shows a high degree

很好　很多

● 行(xíng): 彳+亍(chù)　▶to go; line

\* originally this was a pictograph of a cross road

人行道　银行

</td></tr>
</table>

- 得：彳+旦+寸 ▶ to gain; particle (dé / dàn / cùn)

  \* the radical "彳" means steps, the right side shows one lays his hands on what he has seen

  得到　不得不 (dào)

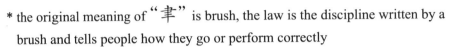

- 律：彳+聿(sound part) ▶ law (lǜ / yù)

  \* the original meaning of "聿" is brush, the law is the discipline written by a brush and tells people how they go or perform correctly

  法律　律师 (fǎ / shī)

- 史：口+乂 ▶ history (shǐ)

  \* the history is always told by people (not exactly "人", "乀" has to go through "丿")

  历史　文学史 (lì)

## Exercises 2（练习二）

1. Choose the correct characters（选择正确的汉字）：

   （1）very　　　　A. 银　　B. 很
   （2）to gain　　　A. 得　　B. 很
   （3）right　　　　A. 对　　B. 双
   （4）history　　　A. 吏　　B. 史
   （5）to guide　　 A. 寻　　B. 导

2. Reading（读一读，认汉字）：

对　不对　对不对　说得对不对　我说得对不对？你说得很对。

导游　要导游　不要导游　要不要导游　我们要一个会说英语的导游。(yóu / yóu / yóu / yóu / yīng / yóu)

很好　说得很好　汉语说得很好　说汉语说得很好　他说汉语说得很好。

自行车　我的自行车　他的自行车　我的自行车很新，他的自行车不新。(zì / zì / zì / zì / xīn / xīn)

银行　银行在哪儿？你知道银行在哪儿吗？银行不在左边，银行在右边。(nǎ / nǎ / biān / biān)

律师　我是律师。　我太太也是律师。　我和太太要学习中国的法律。
lǜshī　　　　shì　　　　　　　　shì　　　　　　　　　　　　　xí　　　fǎ

历史　很长的历史　有很长的历史　中国有很长的历史。
lì shǐ　cháng lì shǐ　　cháng lì shǐ　　　cháng lì shǐ

## III Sound parts
## 声旁

In Chinese characters system, more than 80% are pictophonetic compounds (形声字 xíngshēngzì). This kind of characters usually is made of by two parts, one is the radical, and the other is the sound part. The radical shows the meaning of the character, and the sound part shows the phonetic. To grasp the common sound parts well can make your studying much easier. From this unit, we will introduce one common sound part and the characters with it in each unit.

在汉字系统中，形声字所占的比例超过80%。这类汉字通常由两个部分组成，一是部首，二是声旁。部首表示汉字的意义，声旁表示发音。掌握好常用的声旁可以大大提高汉字学习的效率。从本单元起，我们将在每一单元中介绍一个常用声旁及若干包含该声旁的汉字。

主 (zhǔ) main + 亻 = 住 (zhù) to live　　同住

　　　　　　 + 扌 = 拄 (zhǔ) to support　拄着 (zhe)

　　　　　　 + 氵 = 注 (zhù) to pour　　注水

　　　　　　 + 木 = 柱 (zhù) pillar　　　柱子

### Exercises 3 (练习三)

1. Combine the radicals and the sound part into characters, then match their English meaning (用所给部首和声旁组成汉字并与英文匹配):

   扌　　　　　　　pillar
   氵　　主　　　　to pour
   木　　　　　　　to live
   亻　　　　　　　to support

2. Please write down other characters with this sound part（用上面的声旁再组几个汉字）：

_____

## IV  Homework
## 课后作业

1. Choose the correct radicals（选择正确的偏旁）：

（1）wèi (position)      A. 亻    B. 彳
（2）xíng (to go)         A. 亻    B. 彳
（3）zhù (to live)        A. 亻    B. 彳
（4）yào (to want)        A. 人    B. 女
（5）dǎo (to lead)        A. 扌    B. 寸
（6）zhù (pillar)         A. 扌    B. 木

2. Find the correct pinyin and meaning for the given characters（找找所给汉字正确的拼音和意思）：

对    会    行    信    住    位

huì   duì   xìn   xíng   wèi   zhù

3. Circle the phrases with the characters you have learned as many as you can（用所给汉字组成尽可能多的短语）：

| 得 很 对 如 全 化 |
| 好 大 小 不 要 银 |
| 几 姐 信 会 行 导 |
| 位 史 开 始 律 游 |

1. __很好__    2. _____    3. _____
4. _____   5. _____    6. _____
7. _____   8. _____    9. _____
10. _____   11. _____   12. _____
13. _____   14. _____   15. _____

## 4. Read the following paragraph (读一读，认汉字)：

贝西是英国人。她是去年九月来上海的。她是律师。来上海以后，因为想了解中国的历史、文化和法律，所以她开始学习汉语。从星期一到星期五，她每天上午在大学学习，下午去公司工作。一边工作一边学习汉语非常累。有时候，晚上她去酒吧放松一下。今天晚上，她在酒吧认识了一个新朋友李大明。李大明是马克的好朋友，也是他的汉语辅导老师。李大明说如果贝西有问题可以问他。贝西听了以后非常高兴。

## 5. Writing (写汉字)：

(1) 人 人 会 会 会 会 — 会

(2) 亻 亻 亻 亻 位 位 位 — 位

(3) 亻 亻 亻 亻 亻 信 信 信 — 信

(4) 人 人 全 全 全 全 — 全

(5) 亻 亻 化 化 — 化

# Chinese with Me: A Chinese Character Course Book(II)

丿 亻 亻 仁 件 件 (6)
件 件 件 件 件

𡿨 𡿨 女 如 如 如 姐 姐 (7)
姐 姐 姐 姐 姐

𡿨 𡿨 女 如 如 如 (8)
如 如 如 如 如

𡿨 𡿨 女 女 如 始 始 始 (9)
始 始 始 始 始

一 亓 西 西 西 要 要 要 (10)
要 要 要 要 要

一 十 寸 (11)
寸 寸 寸 寸 寸

又 又 对 对 对 (12)
对 对 对 对 对

っ 已 巳 导 导 导 (13)
导 导 导 导 导

# Unit 16

ノ 彳 彳 彳 彳 彳 很 很 很 (14)

很 很 很 很 很

ノ 彳 彳 彳 行 行 (15)

行 行 行 行 行

ノ 彳 彳 彳 彳 彳 彳 得 得 得 (16)

得 得 得 得 得

ノ 彳 彳 彳 彳 彳 律 律 (17)

律 律 律 律 律

丨 口 口 史 史 (18)

史 史 史 史 史

丶 亠 亠 主 主 (19)

主 主 主 主 主

亻 亻 亻 亻 住 住 住 (20)

住 住 住 住 住

一 十 扌 扌 扌 扫 挂 挂 (21)

挂 挂 挂 挂 挂

*Chinese with Me: A Chinese Character Course Book(II)*

丶 氵 氵 沪 沪 注 注 注 (22)
注 注 注 注 注

十 十 才 术 术 杧 柱 柱 柱 (23)
柱 柱 柱 柱 柱

## 6. Making flash cards (做汉字卡片):

Using flash cards is an effective method to memorize Chinese characters.
Why not make some by yourself? A sample card is shown below.

会

huì

to meet, meeting; can

开会, 大会

　　Side A　　　　　　　　Side B

# Unit 17

## I  Old radicals and new characters
### 旧部首和新汉字

| 冫 |
|---|
| liǎng diǎn shuǐ |
| 两点水 |
| ice |

- 净:冫+争(sound part) ▶clean  
  \* it used to be the name of the moat in front of "Zheng(争) Gate"  
  干净　净土

- 冬:夂(sound part)+冫 ▶winter  
  \* winter is as cold as ice  
  冬天　冬季

| 氵 |
|---|
| sān diǎn shuǐ |
| 三点水 |
| water |

- 汽:氵+气(sound part) ▶steam  
  \* steam is the air with water  
  汽车　汽水

- 港:氵+巷(sound part) ▶harbor  
  \* harbor is always near the water  
  港口　香港

- 酒:氵+酉(sound part) ▶alcohol  
  \* "酉" is a pictograph of an amphora used for distilling, the radical "氵" added to it indicates the jar is filled with the liquor  
  酒杯　白酒

- 法:氵+去 ▶law; French  
  \* as water removes(去) dirt, law removes the vices  
  法律　法国

- 潮：氵+朝(sound part) ▶tide
  * tide is the periodic rise and fall of the sea lexel under the gravitational pull of the moon(月)
  
  潮水　热潮

- 湿：氵+显(日+业) ▶wet
  * the apparent(显) water is wet
  
  潮湿　湿地

- 温：氵+昷(sound part, 日+皿) ▶warm
  * the sun(日) shines on the utensil(皿) to keep the water(氵) warm, and it used to be the name of "Wen River"
  
  室温　温室

- 沿：氵+几+口 ▶along
  * several(几) people(口) float downstream(氵)
  
  沿海　沿着

## Exercises 1（练习一）

1. Choose the correct characters（选择正确的汉字）:

   1. winter　　A. 冬　　B. 各
   2. alcohol　　A. 洒　　B. 酒
   3. law　　A. 去　　B. 法
   4. wet　　A. 潮　　B. 湿
   5. warm　　A. 温　　B. 湿

2. Reading（读一读，认汉字）:

   干净　不干净　很干净　干净不干净　我的家很干净,他的家不干净。

   冬天　冬天很冷　十二月到二月是上海的冬天,上海的冬天很冷。

   汽车　公共汽车　坐公共汽车　坐公共汽车去公司　我每天坐公共汽车去公司。

   香港　香港的港口　香港的港口很忙　香港的港口每天很忙。

   喝酒　会喝酒　很会喝酒　不会喝酒　不太会喝酒　我不太会喝酒。

法语　语法　法语的语法　法语的语法很难(nán)　法语的语法很难(nán)很难(nán)。
潮湿　很潮湿　上海(hǎi)的夏(xià)天很潮湿,北京的夏(xià)天不潮湿。
气(qì)温　最(zuì)高气(qì)温　最(zuì)低(dī)气(qì)温　今天的最(zuì)高气(qì)温是三十度(dù),最(zuì)低(dī)气(qì)温是二十二度(dù)。
沿(hǎi)海　沿(hǎi)海城(shì)市　上(hǎi)海是沿(hǎi)海城(shì)市　上(hǎi)海是中国的沿(hǎi)海城(shì)市。

## II  New radicals and characters
### 新部首和新汉字

| | |
|---|---|
| **气** (qì)<br>气字头 (qì zì tóu)<br>air | ● 气 (qì) : air<br>\* it represents curling vapours rising and forming clouds<br>\* 天气, 气温 |
| **穴** (xué)<br>穴字头 (xué zì tóu)<br>cave | ● 空/空 (kōng/kòng) : 穴 + 工 (sound part) ▶ empty; free time<br>\* a cave is empty when it was excavated by a labour; and it also means a labour is at leisure or free from work<br>空气 (kōng qì)　有空 (yǒu kòng) |
| **雨** (yǔ)<br>雨字头 (yǔ zì tóu)<br>rain | ● 雨 (yǔ) : rain<br>\* raindrops( ;; ) fall vertically down( ｜ ) from a cloud( 冂 ) in the heavens(一)<br>\* 大雨, 下雨<br><br>● 雪 (xuě) : 雨 + 彐 (jì) ▶ snow<br>\* the rain which can be taken up in a hand is snow<br>下雪　雪花 (xuě huā)<br><br>● 零 (líng) : 雨 + 令 (líng) (sound part) ▶ zero<br>\* its original meaning is drizzle<br>零钱　找零 |

<table>
<tr><td>

zhuī
**隹**

cuī zì páng
**隹字旁**
bird

</td><td>

nán yòu
- **难**: 又+隹 ▶difficult

  \* it is difficult to catch a bird by a hand; or it is difficult to escape for a bird when it is caught by a hand

  kùn
  困难   难题

</td></tr>
</table>

jí mù
- **集**: 隹+木 ▶to gather

  \* birds like to gather on the tree. The ancient character shows three birds flock together on a tree

  集中   集合

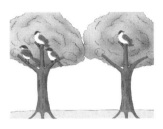

ér
- **而**: moreover, but

  \* originally it refers to the bristles on the jaws

  qiě fǎn
  而且   反而

píng gān
- **平**: 干+ `ヽˊ` ▶flat

  \* " `ヽˊ` " supports the surface and makes it flat

  平时   公平

## Exercises 2（练习二）

1. Choose the correct characters（选择正确的汉字）:

    (1) air         A. 气       B. 汽
    (2) empty       A. 容       B. 空
    (3) zero        A. 零       B. 雪
    (4) to gather   A. 难       B. 集
    (5) but         A. 而       B. 面
    (6) flat        A. 干       B. 平

2. Reading（读一读，认汉字）:

xīn xiān        xīn xiān          zhí xīn xiān              zhí xīn xiān
空气   空气新鲜   空气很新鲜   空气一直很新鲜   那里的空气一直很新鲜。

小雨   下小雨   每天下小雨   这个星期每天下小雨。

大雪　下大雪　明天下大雪　天气预报说明天下大雪。

零　零比零　比分是零比零　今天晚上比赛的比分是零比零。

集中　集中一下　大家集中一下　大家集中一下，我有话要说。

而且　不但……而且……　不但会说汉语　她不但会说汉语而且说得很好。

平时　平时学习很忙　女儿平时学习很忙。　女儿平时学习很忙，很少有时间玩。

## III Sound parts
## 声旁

分 (fēn) to divide + 亻 = 份 (fèn) share, portion　一份

+ 口 = 吩 (fēn) to instruct　吩咐

+ 纟 = 纷 (fēn) numerous　纷纷

+ 气 = 氛 (fēn) atmosphere　气氛

+ 米 = 粉 (fěn) powder　花粉

### Exercises 3（练习三）

1. Combine the radicals and the sound part into characters, then match their English meaning（用所给部首和声旁组成汉字并与英文匹配）：

   口　　　　　powder
   亻　　　　　numerous
   纟　　分　　atmosphere
   米　　　　　to instruct
   气　　　　　share, portion

2. Please write down other characters with this sound part（用上面的声旁再组几个汉字）：

_____

# IV Homework
## 课后作业

1. Choose the correct radicals:

    (1) jìng (clean)    A. 冫    B. 氵
    (2) qì (steam)      A. 冫    B. 氵
    (3) kōng (empty)    A. 宀    B. 穴
    (4) xuě (snow)      A. 雨    B. 气
    (5) nán (difficult) A. 住    B. 佳
    (6) fěn (powder)    A. 木    B. 米

2. Find the correct pinyin and meaning for the given characters（找找所给汉字正确的拼音和意思）:

   酒           冬           零           雪           港

   jiǔ          dōng         xuě          gǎng         líng

3. Circle the phrases with the characters you have learned as many as you can（用所给汉字组成尽可能多的短语）:

   | 冬 | 天 | 下 | 雪 | 港 | 口 |
   |---|---|---|---|---|---|
   | 空 | 气 | 雨 | 酒 | 潮 | 湿 |
   | 平 | 干 | 温 | 水 | 集 | 中 |
   | 净 | 时 | 汽 | 零 | 钱 | 难 |

   1. 冬天    2. _____    3. _____
   4. _____   5. _____    6. _____
   7. _____   8. _____    9. _____
   10. _____  11. _____   12. _____
   13. _____  14. _____   15. _____

4. Read the following paragraph（读一读,认汉字）:

   上海是中国东部的沿海城市。四季分明。冬夏较长,春秋较短,冬天约有126天,夏天约有110天,春秋两季相加约130天。

上海的年平均气温16℃左右。7、8月气温最高,月平均约28℃;1月最低,月平均约4℃。

上海的年平均降雨量在1200毫米左右,但一年中60%的雨量集中在5到10月。上海的夏天比较潮湿,冬天很少下雪。

## 5. Writing (写汉字):

丶 冫 冫 冹 冹 浄 浄 净 净 (24)
净 净 净 净 净

夂 冬 冬 冬 冬 (25)
冬 冬 冬 冬 冬

丶 冫 冫 汒 汽 汽 汽 (26)
汽 汽 汽 汽 汽

丶 冫 冫 汢 汢 洪 洪 洪 洪 港 港 港 (27)
港 港 港 港 港

丶 冫 冫 汀 沂 沂 洒 酒 酒 酒 (28)
酒 酒 酒 酒 酒

丶 冫 冫 汁 法 法 法 (29)
法 法 法 法 法

丶 氵 氵 氵 汁 汁 泸 泸 泔 淖 淖 潮 潮 潮 潮 (30)

潮 潮 潮 潮 潮

丶 氵 氵 氵 沪 沪 浔 浔 淠 湿 湿 湿 (31)

湿 湿 湿 湿 湿

丶 氵 氵 沪 沪 沪 泥 浔 温 温 温 温 (32)

温 温 温 温 温

丶 氵 氵 沪 汎 沿 沿 沿 (33)

沿 沿 沿 沿 沿

丿 乞 气 气 (34)

气 气 气 气 气

丶 宀 宀 穴 穴 (35)

穴 穴 穴 穴 穴

丶 宀 宀 穴 穴 窄 空 空 (36)

空 空 空 空 空

一 冂 冂 币 币 雨 雨 雨 (37)

雨 雨 雨 雨 雨

# Unit 17

一 宀 丙 而 雨 雨 雪 雪 雪 雪 (38)

雪 雪 雪 雪 雪

一 宀 丙 而 雨 雨 雨 零 零 零 零 零 (39)

零 零 零 零 零

丿 亻 亻 亻 仁 仨 佳 佳 (40)

佳 佳 佳 佳 佳

又 又 刈 刈 邓 难 难 难 难 (41)

难 难 难 难 难

丿 亻 亻 亻 仁 仨 佳 佳 隹 集 集 集 (42)

集 集 集 集 集

一 丆 丙 而 而 而 (43)

而 而 而 而 而

一 宀 六 平 平 (44)

平 平 平 平 平

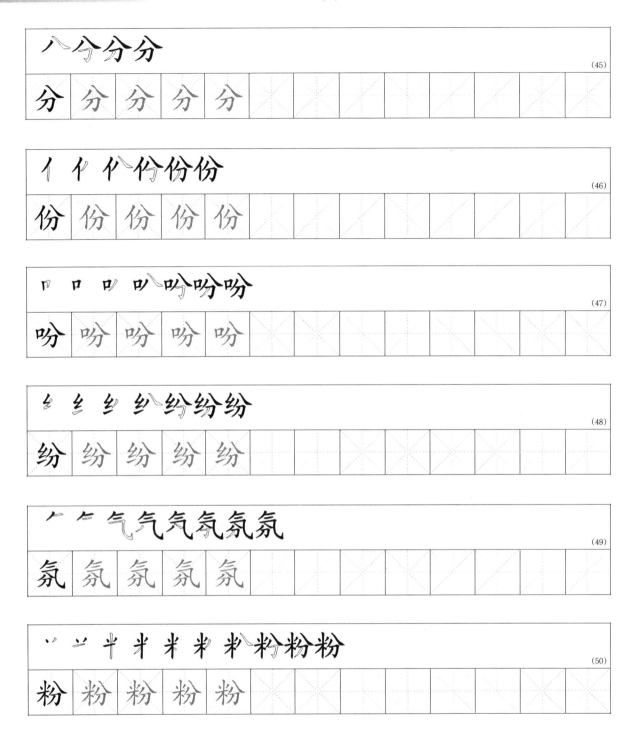

6. Making flash cards (做汉字卡片)。

# Unit 18

## 1 Old radicals and new characters
### 旧部首和新汉字

| kǒu |
|---|
| 口 |
| kǒu zì páng |
| 口字旁 |
| mouth |

- 哪(nǎ)：口＋那(sound part) ▶which

  \* using mouth（口）to ask questions

  哪个(nǎ)　哪里(nǎ)

- 号/號(háo/hào)：口＋丂(yú) ▶to shout; number

  \* it comes from mouth uttering an exclamation

  号叫(háo)　记号(hào)

- 吐/吐(tǔ/tù)：口＋土(tǔ)(sound part) ▶to spit; to vomit

  \* to spit out the duat（土）from the mouth（口）

  吐气(tǔ)　吐血(tù xiě)

- 吸(xī)：口＋及(jí)(sound part) ▶to breathe in

  \* feel the air or smoke and breathe into the mouth（口）

  吸气　吸烟

| huǒ |
|---|
| 火 |
| huǒ zì páng |
| 火字旁 |
| sì diǎn dǐ |
| (灬—四点底) |
| fire |

- 燥(zào)：火＋品(pǐn)＋木(mù) ▶dry

  \* putting something on the wood, then using fire to make it dry

  干燥　燥热

- 炼(liàn)：火＋东(not 东) ▶to refine

  \* to refine things by fire（火）

  炼钢(gāng)　锻炼(duàn)

23

## Exercises 1 (练习一)

1. Choose the correct characters (选择正确的汉字):

(1) which      A. 那    B. 哪

(2) number      A. 号    B. 另

(3) to vomit      A. 吐    B. 叶

(4) to breathe in      A. 吃    B. 吸

(5) to refine      A. 东    B. 炼

2. Reading (读一读,认汉字):

哪国　哪国人　你是哪国人？　哪里　你住在哪里？　你在哪里工作？

几号　星期几　几月几号　今天是几月几号星期几？　今天是四月十号星期三。

tán　　　suí　　tán　　　suí　　tán　　　　suí　　tán
吐痰　随地吐痰　不要随地吐痰　请不要随地吐痰。

néng　　néng　　　gòng　suǒ néng　　xiē　suǒ néng
吸烟　能吸烟　不能吸烟　公共场所不能吸烟　有些公共场所不能吸烟。

jīng　hǎi　jīng　hǎi
干燥　北京干燥　上海不干燥　北京的天气比上海干燥。

duàn　měi duàn　　hǎi qián měi duàn　　hǎi hòu měi duàn
锻炼　每天锻炼　来上海以前我每天锻炼,来上海以后我不每天锻炼了。

# II New radicals and characters
## 新部首和新汉字

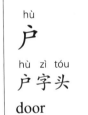

户
hù zì tóu
户字头
door

● 户 hù: door; a household or family

\* it is a pictograph of a one-leafed door, and used as a radical relating to doors and spaces

门户　户主

● 所 suǒ : 户 + 斤 (jīn) ▶ place

\* it shows the place where chops the firewood with the axe is near the house

场所　所以

● 房 fáng : 户 + 方 (fāng) (sound part) ▶ house; room

\* every house has doors (户)

房子　房间

24

# Unit 18

| 疒 |
|---|
| bìng zì tóu |
| 病字头 |
| illness |

- 病：疒 + 丙(sound part) ▶illness
  
  病人　病房

| 足(𧾷) |
|---|
| zú |
| zú zì páng |
| 足字旁 |
| foot |

- 足：口 + 止 ▶foot
  
  * the top square shows the knee, and the down part is the foot
  
  平足　手足

- 路：足 + 各 ▶road
  
  * road is a path to each（各）direction
  
  路口　公路

- 跟：足 + 艮(sound part) ▶heel; to follow
  
  * the right part "艮" is not only a sound part but also a meaning part, it originally means the limitation or the border, so the border of foot is heel
  
  高跟　跟上

- 跑：足 + 包(sound part) ▶to run
  
  * running by feet
  
  快跑　跑车

- 其：he, she, it
  
  其他　其中

- 身：body
  
  * it pictures a human figure with prominent belly and one leg goes forward to support the body
  
  身高　身体

- 失：to lose
  
  失去　失言

- 首：first
  
  * its original meaning is head, the top " ˇ " represents hair, "一" represents scalp, and the "目" of course represents eyes
  
  首先　首要

- 至 (zhì): at
  * the original form is a pictograph of a bird downwards to the earth
  至少　至多
- 于 (yú): at
  至于　于是

## Exercises 2（练习二）

**1. Choose the correct characters（选择正确的汉字）:**

（1）place　　A. 所　　B. 听
（2）road　　 A. 路　　B. 跟　　C. 跑
（3）body　　 A. 其　　B. 身　　C. 首
（4）to lose　 A. 夭　　B. 夫　　C. 失
（5）at　　　 A. 干　　B. 于　　C. 平

**2. Reading（读一读，认汉字）:**

户口　上海户口　有没有上海户口？　我没有上海户口。
　　　因为我没有上海户口，所以我要办(bàn)一个上海户口。

房间　几个房间　有几个房间　有几个房间朝(cháo)南　这个房子有几个房间朝(cháo)南？

生病　没生病　我没生病　我没生病，就(jiù)是不太舒(shū)服。

路口　十字路口　下一个十字路口　下一个十字路口左拐(guǎi)。

跟我一起　她跟我一起　她跟我一起去商(shāng)店　她跟我一起去商(shāng)店买东西。

跑步(bù)　跑得快　跑步(bù)跑得很快　他跑步(bù)跑得比我快得多。

其他　其他同学　其他同学是西方人　我是日本人，其他同学是西方人。

身体　身体很好　你的身体会很好　如果每(měi)天早睡(shuì)早起，你的身体就会很好。

失去　不想失去　我不想失去你　我不想失去你这个朋友。

首先　首先……其次(cì)……　首先……其次(cì)……最后(zuì hòu)……

至于　至于去哪里我还没决(jué)定(dìng)　下个月我想去旅(lǚ)行，至于去哪里我还没决(jué)定(dìng)。

## III  Sound parts
## 声旁

fāng  
方 square +   

fǎng  
亻 = 仿 to imitate   

gǔ  
仿古

fǎng  
+ 讠 = 访 to visit   

访问

fǎng  
+ 纟 = 纺 to spin   

zhī  
纺织

fáng  
+ 女 = 妨 to harm   

ài  
妨碍

### Exercises 3 (练习三)

1. Combine the radicals and the sound part into characters, then match their English meaning (用所给部首和声旁组成汉字并与英文匹配):

   户            to harm
   纟            house
   讠      方    to spin
   女            to visit
   亻            to imitate

2. Please write down other characters with this sound part (用上面的声旁再组几个汉字):

_____

## IV  Homework
## 课后作业

1. Choose the correct radicals (选择正确的偏旁):

   (1) zào (dry)            A. 氵    B. 火
   (2) liàn (to refine)     A. 火    B. 纟
   (3) fáng (house)         A. 尸    B. 户
   (4) gēn (heel)           A. 彳    B. 足
   (5) pǎo (to run)         A. 扌    B. 足
   (6) fǎng (to imitate)    A. 亻    B. 彳

2. Find the correct pinyin and meaning for the given characters（找找所给汉字正确的拼音和意思）：

病　　　　　　房　　　　　　路　　　　　　号　　　　　　跑

hào　　　　　lù　　　　　bìng　　　　　fáng　　　　　pǎo

3. Circle the phrases with the characters you have learned as many as you can（用所给汉字组成尽可能多的短语）：

| 哪里 | 所 | 有 | 房 | 生 |
|---|---|---|---|---|
| 儿 | 几 | 路 | 以 | 子 | 病 |
| 号 | 首 | 先 | 身 | 其 | 人 |
| 失 | 去 | 至 | 于 | 体 | 中 |

1. 哪里　　　2. _____　　　3. _____
4. _____　　4. _____　　5. _____　　6. _____
7. _____　　8. _____　　9. _____
10. _____　　11. _____　　12. _____
13. _____　　14. _____　　15. _____

4. Read the following paragraph（读一读，认汉字）：

　　中国有句俗(sú)语叫"早睡(shuì)早起身体好"。意思(yì)是：如果你每天睡(shuì)得早起得早，那(nà)么你的身体就会很好。我觉得这句话说得很对。早一点起床(chuáng)有很多的好处(chù)。首先，早上是运动(yùndòng)的最佳(zuì jiā)时间。中午的休息(xiū xi)时间比较短(jiǎoduǎn)，而且(qiě)很饿(è)或者(huòzhě)很饱(bǎo)的时候都不能锻炼(houdōu néngduàn)。下班(bān)以后(hòu)比较(jiào)累，也可能(néng)有别(bié)的事(shì)，比如去买东西、跟朋友吃饭什么的。至于锻炼的方式，跑步、骑自行车、游泳或者(duàn shì bù qí zì yóuyǒnghuòzhě)去健身房，都(jiàn dōu)是很好的运动(yùndòng)。其次(cì)，早点出门的话，路上不堵(dǔ)车，也有很多的空出租(zū)车。这样(yàng)，从我家到(dào)学校(xiào)，只要很短(duǎn)的时间。同学们一般(bān)不会太早来学校(xiào)，所以教(jiào)室里很安静(ān jìng)。我一边喝咖啡(biān hē kā fēi)，一边(biān)学(xí)习汉语，没有人打扰(rǎo)我，学(xiào)习的效率(lǜ)非常(fēicháng)高。

5. Writing (写汉字):

厂 F F F 所 所 所 所 (58)

所 所 所 所 所

丶 亠 户 户 户 房 房 房 (59)

房 房 房 房 房

丶 广 广 疒 疒 (60)

疒 疒 疒 疒 疒

丶 广 广 疒 疒 疒 病 病 病 病 (61)

病 病 病 病 病

口 口 口 甲 甲 足 足 (62)

足 足 足 足 足

口 口 口 甲 甲 趴 趴 趵 路 路 路 (63)

路 路 路 路 路

口 口 口 甲 甲 趴 趴 趴 跟 跟 跟 (64)

跟 跟 跟 跟 跟

口 口 口 甲 甲 趴 趴 趵 跑 跑 (65)

跑 跑 跑 跑 跑

# Unit 18

一 十 卄 甘 其 其 其 其 (66)

其 其 其 其 其

丿 亻 亻 自 自 身 身 (67)

身 身 身 身 身

丿 一 牛 失 失 (68)

失 失 失 失 失

丶 丷 亼 产 首 首 首 首 首 (69)

首 首 首 首 首

二 于 于 (70)

于 于 于 于 于

一 工 互 至 至 至 (71)

至 至 至 至 至

丶 亠 方 方 (72)

方 方 方 方 方

丿 亻 仁 伫 仿 仿 (73)

仿 仿 仿 仿 仿

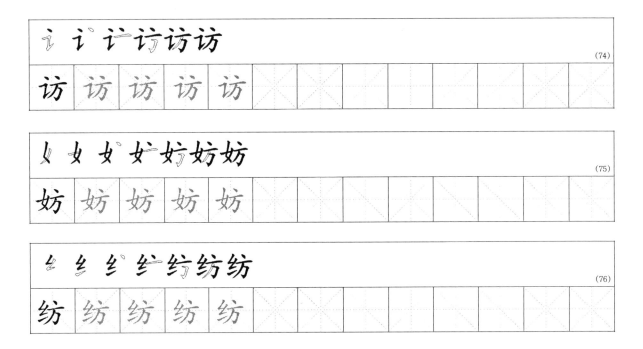

6. Making flash cards (做汉字卡片)。

# Unit 19

## I Old radicals and new characters
### 旧部首和新汉字

**辶**
zǒu zhī dǐ
走之底
walk

- 过：辶+寸 ▶to pass
  * the link on the carriage makes the carriage moving
  过去　过年

- 边：辶+力 ▶side
  右边　身边

- 送：辶+关 ▶to deliver; to see somebody off
  送信　送行

- 运：辶+云 (sound part) ▶to transport
  运送　运行

- 连：辶+车 ▶to link
  * the link on the carriage makes the carriage moving
  连日　相连

- 退：辶+艮 ▶to move back; to return
  退路　退还

- 通：辶+甬 (sound part) ▶through
  通过　交通

**广**
guǎng
guǎngzì tóu
广字头
wide

- 度：广+廿+又 ▶degree; to spend (time)
  * people use their hands(又) to measure during the ancient time
  温度　度过

33

- 应/应：广 + 丷　▶should; to respond
  
  应该　答应
  <sub>yīng</sub>　<sub>dā yìng</sub>

## Exercises 1（练习一）

1. Choose the correct characters（选择正确的汉字）:

   1. to pass　　　A. 过　　B. 还
   2. side　　　　A. 辺　　B. 边
   3. to transport　A. 运　　B. 远
   4. degree　　　A. 库　　B. 度
   5. should　　　A. 应　　B. 庄

2. Reading（读一读，认汉字）:

   过年　回家过年　应该回家过年　春节应该回家过年。

   一边　一边吃晚饭　一边吃晚饭一边看电视　我常常一边吃晚饭一边看电视。

   送　送你　送你回家　开车送你回家　我开车送你回家吧。

   连　连老师　连老师也不知道　这个问题太难了，连老师也不知道。

   退票　退票容易　退票容易买票难。

   度　三十七度　体温是三十七度　人的正常体温是三十七度。

   答应　答应别人　答应了别人　答应了别人就一定要做到。

# II New radicals and characters
## 新部首和新汉字

**力**
lì zì páng
力字旁
strength

- 力: strength, power
  * it is a powerful graphic impression of a forearm with muscle
  
  有气　有力

34

# Unit 19

- 助: 且(sound part)＋力 ▶ to help

  \* giving strength to the person you want to help

  助手　助跑

- 动: 云＋力 ▶ to move

  \* using strength to make the clouds move

  运动　动力

- 办: 力＋ノヽ ▶ to handle

  \* the problem can be handled by someone's strength (ノ) and friends' help (ヽ)

  办公室　怎么办

- 加: 力＋口 ▶ to add

  \* it adds strength to mouth by applying force to words

  加号　加油

| zhǐ |
|---|
| 止 |
| zhǐ zì páng |
| 止字旁 |
| stop |

- 正/正: 一＋止 ▶ the first month of the lunar year; correctitude

  \* it is an ideograph of a foot walking in a straight line

  正月　正在

- 步: 止＋少 (not 少) ▶ step

  \* it is an ideograph of a right foot and a left foot, one following the other, conveying the idea of walking steps

  步行　退步

| zhōu |
|---|
| 舟 |
| zhōu zì páng |
| 舟字旁 |
| boat |

- 航: 舟＋亢(sound part) ▶ to sail

  航行　航空

- 父: father

  \* it looks like two sticks in hands for blaming the kids

  父子　父女

- 母: mother

  \* it is a picture of woman with breasts for suckling a child

  父母　母牛

35

## Chinese with Me: A Chinese Character Course Book(II)

- 每: ⼂+母 ▶every (měi, mǔ)

  每天　每个

- 海: 氵+每 ▶sea (hǎi, měi)

  \* the water covers every inch, no doubt, it is sea

  上海　海运

## Exercises 2 (练习二)

1. Choose the correct characters (选择正确的汉字):

   (1) to do　　　A. 办　B. 为
   (2) to add　　 A. 加　B. 咖
   (3) to stop　　A. 止　B. 正
   (4) step　　　 A. 步　B. 歩
   (5) mother　　A. 毋　B. 母
   (6) every　　　A. 母　B. 每

2. Reading (读一读,认汉字):

   帮助(bāng)　帮助过我(bāng)　帮助过我的人(bāng)　我要感谢帮助过我的人(gǎn xiè bāng)。

   运动　喜欢的运动(xǐ huan)　最喜欢的运动(zuì xǐ huan)　我最喜欢的运动(zuì xǐ huan)

   我最喜欢的运动是跑步(zuì xǐ huan)。

   办公室　在办公室　在办公室加班(bān)　王先生还在办公室加班吗(bān)?

   正在　正在上课　正在上汉语课　现在正在上汉语课

   我们现在正在上汉语课。

   航空　航空公司　在航空公司工作　我的父母都(dōu)在航空公司工作。

   每个　每个同学　每个同学介绍一下(jiè shào)　请(qǐng)每个同学介绍一下自己(jiè shào zì jǐ)。

   海边　在海边　在海边长大(zhǎng)　从小在海边长大(zhǎng)　我从小在海边长大(zhǎng)。

## III  Sound parts
### 声旁

bā      bǎ
巴 cling to + 扌 = 把 to hold    把手

            ba
       + 口 = 吧 a particle    酒吧

            bà
       + 父 = 爸 father    爸爸

            bā        shāng
       + 疒 = 疤 scar    伤疤

### Exercises 3（练习三）

1. Combine the radicals and the sound part into characters, then match their English meaning（用所给部首和声旁组成汉字并与英文匹配）:

    扌                       father
    疒                       scar
    父      巴
                              to hold
    口                       a particle

2. Please write down other characters with this sound part（用上面的声旁再组几个汉字）:

_____

## IV  Homework
### 课后作业

1. Choose the correct radicals（选择正确的偏旁）:

     (1) tuì (to move back)       A. 辶    B. 足

     (2) dù (degree)             A. 厂    B. 广

     (3) dòng (to move)         A. 辶    B. 力

     (4) háng (to sail)           A. 彳    B. 舟

     (5) hǎi (sea)                A. 冫    B. 氵

     (6) bǎ (to hold)            A. 扌    B. 口

2. Find the correct pinyin and meaning for the given characters（找找所给汉字正确的拼音和意思）:

航　　　度　　　步　　　爸　　　加　　　海

dù　　　bù　　　bà　　　jiā　　　hǎi　　　háng

3. Circle the phrases with the characters you have learned as many as you can（用所给汉字组成尽可能多的短语）:

父母每天送运
正步航海行动
退刀一边加会
疤度过办公法

1. 父母　　　2. _____　　　3. _____
4. _____　　　5. _____　　　6. _____
7. _____　　　8. _____　　　9. _____
10. _____　　11. _____　　12. _____
13. _____　　14. _____　　15. _____

4. Read the following paragraph（读一读,认汉字）:

　　　　　chūn jié wáng gāng　　　　　　　jīn　　 dā　　　　　　　dìng　　　　　　　wèi chūn jié
去年春节王 刚没有回家。今年他答应父母一定回家过年。因为春节
qián　piào　mǎi　　　wáng gāng　　　jiù yù　　　zhāng piào　　　　xiào tū rán　jí
前的票很难买,所以王 刚很早就预订好了一张火车票。可是,学校突然有急
shì　　　　wáng gāng　diào yuán mǎi　　piào dàn　　zài mǎi　zhāng jiù kùn
事,要晚两天走。王 刚只好退掉了原来买的火车票,但是要再买一张就困难
　　wáng gāng　diàn　　lǐ　　qǐng bāng máng　lǐ
了。王 刚打电话给李大明请他帮 忙。李大明说他认识在航空公司工作的
　　　　　néng　　mǎi dào fēi　piào　　　　　　lǐ　　　　diàn　wáng gāng　　　　　bāng
朋友,可能可以买到飞机票。下午,李大明打电话给王 刚,说他的朋友帮
wáng gāng mǎi dào　fēi　piào dàn　néng　zhé piào　　　guì　wáng gāng　　xi　　néng
王 刚买到了飞机票,但是不能打折,票价有点儿贵。王 刚说没关系,只要能
　　　jiù
回家就好。

5. Writing (写汉字):

丶 广 广 庐 庐 度 度 度 度 (84)

度 度 度 度 度

丶 广 广 广 庐 应 应 应 (85)

应 应 应 应 应

力 力 (86)

力 力 力 力 力

丨 冂 月 月 目 助 助 (87)

助 助 助 助 助

二 云 云 云 动 动 (88)

动 动 动 动 动

力 力 办 办 (89)

办 办 办 办 办

力 力 加 加 加 (90)

加 加 加 加 加

Unit 19

| 卜 | 卜 | 止 | 止 | | | | | | | | |

止 止 止 止 止

(91)

丁 下 下 正 正

正 正 正 正 正

(92)

卜 止 止 步 步 步 步

步 步 步 步 步

(93)

丿 几 几 舟 舟 舟

舟 舟 舟 舟 舟

(94)

丿 几 几 舟 舟 舟 舟 舟 航 航

航 航 航 航 航

(95)

八 八 父 父

父 父 父 父 父

(96)

口 母 母 母 母

母 母 母 母 母

(97)

41

# Chinese with Me: A Chinese Character Course Book(II)

丿 𠂉 每 每 每 每 每 (98)

每 每 每 每 每

丶 丶 氵 汁 汁 海 海 海 海 海 (99)

海 海 海 海 海

フ ㄋ 巴 巴 (100)

巴 巴 巴 巴 巴

一 扌 扌 扌 扌 把 把 (101)

把 把 把 把 把

丨 口 口 吅 吅 吧 吧 (102)

吧 吧 吧 吧 吧

丿 丷 父 父 爷 爷 爸 爸 (103)

爸 爸 爸 爸 爸

丶 亠 广 广 疒 疒 疒 疤 疤 (104)

疤 疤 疤 疤 疤

6. Making flash cards（做汉字卡片）。

# Unit 20

## I  Old radicals and new characters
### 旧部首和新汉字

| chē<br>车<br>chē zì páng<br>车字旁<br>vehicle |
|---|

- 辅：车+甫(sound part) ▶to assist
  <sub>fǔ     fǔ</sub>
  * the original meaning is "side poles of cart", which assists the cart
  辅导　辅助

- 轻：车+圣(sound part) ▶light
  <sub>qīng   jīng</sub>
  * the original meaning of this character is a light cart, therefore it has the radical "车"
  轻便　年轻

- 轨：车+九 ▶rail; track
  <sub>guǐ    jiǔ</sub>
  * the original meaning of this character is the distance between two wheels
  铁轨　轻轨

- 较：车+交(sound part) ▶to compare
  <sub>jiào   jiāo</sub>
  * the war chariots of two sides neet(交)and fight to see which side is the winner
  比较　较大

| zǒu<br>走<br>zǒu zì páng<br>走字旁<br>walk |
|---|

- 超：走+召(sound part) ▶to surpass; super
  <sub>chāo   zhào</sub>
  超过　超人

- 越：走+戉(sound part) ▶to exceed
  <sub>yuè    yuè</sub>
  超越　越来越

| tián<br>田<br>tián zì páng<br>田字旁<br>field |
|---|

- 累：田+糸 ▶tired
  <sub>lèi    mì</sub>
  * man is working in the field(田), woman is weaving the silk(糸), they are both tired
  心累　劳累
  <sub>     láo</sub>

- 由 (yóu) : because
  * the original meaning is to sprout, and it just looks like a seedling is coming out

  由于　理由(lǐ)

- 电 (diàn) : lightening, electricity
  * the lightening usually comes together with the heavy rain, so the traditional character has the radical of rain(雨), the simplified one shows the lightening is coming down over the field

  电灯　电话

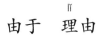

## Exercises 1（练习一）

**1. Choose the correct characters（选择正确的汉字）:**

（1）to assist　　　A. 辆　　B. 辅
（2）light　　　　　A. 轻　　B. 轨
（3）super　　　　 A. 超　　B. 越
（4）tired　　　　　A. 畏　　B. 累
（5）electricity　　 A. 田　　B. 由　　C. 电

**2. Reading（读一读，认汉字）:**

辅导　辅导老师(lǎo shī)　汉语辅导老师(lǎo shī)　找汉语辅导老师(lǎo shī)

我要找一个汉语辅导老师(lǎo shī)。

轻轨　坐轻轨　坐轻轨去学校(xiào)　我坐轻轨去学校(xiào)

我每天早上坐轻轨去学校(xiào)。

超市(shì)　一家超市(shì)　有一家大超市(shì)　附(fù)近有一家大超市(shì)

我家附(fù)近有一家大超市。

越来越　越来越好　写得越来越好　你的汉字写得越来越好了。

累　不累　不太累　太累了　不要太累　工作不要太累。

由于　由于努力(nǔ)　由于大家的努力(nǔ)　由于大家的努力(nǔ)，工作提(tí)前完(wán)成(chéng)了。

电话　打电话　接电话（jiē）　挂电话（guà）　电话忙

## II New radicals and characters
### 新部首和新汉字

| yòu<br>又<br>yòu zì páng<br>又字旁<br>right hand |
|---|

- 反（fǎn）：厂(sound part)＋又（hàn） ▶to turn over
  * its original meaning is to turn over the hands(又)
  
  相反　反对

- 发（fā）：to send out; hair
  * its original meaning is to shoot an arrow
  
  发生　头发（tóu）

| fǎn<br>夂<br>fǎn wén páng<br>反文旁<br>a hand with a stick |
|---|

- 放（fàng）：方(sound part)＋夂（fāng） ▶to put; to release
  * it means to drive out(夂) into an open space(方)
  
  放下　发放

- 效（xiào）：交(sound part)＋夂（jiāo） ▶effect
  
  效果　有效

- 改（gǎi）：己（jǐ）＋夂 ▶to change
  * holding a stick to spur oneself to improve
  
  改名　改道

- 收（shōu）：＋夂 ▶to receive
  
  收信　收回

- 前（qián）：front
  
  前天　以前

- 亲（qīn）：立＋木（lì） ▶in person
  
  亲口　亲手

Unit 20

45

## Chinese with Me: A Chinese Character Course Book(II)

• 自 (zì)：

\* it is a pictographic representation of a nose because the gesture of pointing at one's nose in China means the person himself

亲自　自我

## Exercises 2 (练习二)

### 1. Choose the correct characters (选择正确的汉字):

1. to turn over　　A. 反　　B. 后
2. hair　　　　　　A. 友　　B. 发
3. to put　　　　　A. 放　　B. 效
4. front　　　　　A. 前　　B. 削
5. self　　　　　　A. 日　　B. 目　　C. 自

### 2. Reading (读一读，认汉字):

反　相反　跟你的相反　我的想法跟你的相反。

发信　发给你的信　我发给你的信　我发给你的信你收到了吗？

放　放在哪里　放在那里　这些东西放在哪里？这些东西放在那里。
　　　　　　　　　　　　　　　　xiē　　　　　　　　　xiē

效率　工作效率　工作效率很高　小王的工作效率很高。
lǜ　　　lǜ　　　　lǜ　　　　　　　　lǜ

改　改名字　改了名字　最近改了名字　那家公司最近改了名字。
　　　　　　　　　　　zuì　　　　　　　　　zuì

前面　前面是我的家　前面就是我的家，不用送了。
miàn　miàn　　　　miàn jiù

亲口　亲口告诉　亲口告诉我　他亲口告诉我　这是他亲口告诉我的。
　　　gào sù　　gào sù　　　gào sù　　　　gào sù

自己　自己的事情　自己的事情应该自己去做。
　　　shì qing　shì qing　　　zuò

## III Sound parts
## 声旁

正 straight (zhèng) + 讠(zhèng) = 证 to prove (zhèng)  　　证明

+ 忄 = 怔 to be terrified (zhèng)  　　怔怔

+ 彳 = 征 to go on a journey (zhèng)  　　长征 (cháng)

+ 攵 = 政 politics (zhèng)  　　政治 (zhì)

+ 疒 = 症 disease (zhèng)  　　病症

### Exercises 3（练习三）

1. Combine the radicals and the sound part into characters, then match their English meaning（用所给部首和声旁组成汉字并与英文匹配）:

攵　　　　　　　　disease
彳　　　　　　　　to prove
讠　　　正　　　　politics
疒　　　　　　　　to go on a journey
忄　　　　　　　　to be terrified

2. Please write down other characters with this sound part（用上面的声旁再组几个汉字）:

_____

## IV Homework
## 课后作业

1. Choose the correct radicals（选择正确的偏旁）:

（1）guǐ (rail)　　　　　A. 车　　B. 舟
（2）yuè (to exceed)　　A. 足　　B. 走
（3）fā (to send out)　　A. 又　　B. 攵
（4）gǎi (to change)　　 A. 又　　B. 攵
（5）zhēng (to be terrified) A. 忄　　B. 彳

2. Find the correct pinyin and meaning for the given characters（找找所给汉字正确的拼音和意思）：

累　　　　　　　　发　　　　　　　　电　　　　　　　　轨

fà　　　　　　　　diàn　　　　　　　　lèi　　　　　　　　guǐ

3. Circle the phrases with the characters you have learned as many as you can（用所给汉字组成尽可能多的短语）：

| 辅 轻 轨 发 超 越 |
| 改 导 电 证 人 症 |
| 前 正 放 亲 效 果 |
| 反 面 自 心 由 于 |

1. 辅导　　　　2. _____　　　　3. _____
4. _____　　　5. _____　　　　6. _____
7. _____　　　8. _____　　　　9. _____
10. _____　　 11. _____　　　 12. _____
13. _____　　 14. _____　　　 15. _____

4. Read the following paragraph（读一读，认汉字）：

　　　　　　gé　　　　hòu　　　　　zhǎn　fēicháng　　　　　　　　　　　bān　　bān
　　改革开放以后，上海发展得非常快。以前，人们上班、下班、上学、放学，
guàngjiē　　　　　　qí　　　　jiù　　　　gòng
出门逛街、走亲访友，不是骑自行车就是坐公共汽车。现在不但有了地铁和
　　qiě mǎi sī　　　　　　　　　　　　　　　　　　　　　　　xǐ huan qí
轻轨，而且买私车的人也越来越多了。不过还是有很多人喜欢骑自行车。
qí　　　　　chù　　　　jiào　　　　　　suàn　　　　　　bān jiù　　　dào
骑自行车的好处是时间比较自由。只要算好时间，一般就不会迟到。不但
　　dǔ　　　qiě　　　　duàn　tǐ　　　　　　　　　　　guāfēng　　　　　　jiù
不会堵车，而且还可以锻炼身体。要是天气不好，比如刮风、下雨、下雪，就
jiào má fan　　　　　　jiù qí　　　　　　　　yàng　gòng　　　　　　　jiù
比较麻烦。所以，有的人就不骑自行车了。这样，公共汽车、地铁和轻轨就
　jǐ　　　zū　　　　　　　　　chángcháng　　dào　zū
会比平时挤得多。坐出租车的人也比平时多得多，常　常很难叫到出租车。

5. Writing (写汉字):

土 车 车 车 轩 轩 轩 軿 辅 辅 辅 (105)

辅 辅 辅 辅 辅

土 车 车 车 轩 轻 轻 轻 轻 (106)

轻 轻 轻 轻 轻

土 车 车 轩 轨 轨 (107)

轨 轨 轨 轨 轨

土 车 车 车 车 轩 轩 较 较 较 (108)

较 较 较 较 较

十 土 キ キ キ 走 走 走 赵 越 越 越 (109)

越 越 越 越 越

十 土 キ キ キ 走 走 起 起 超 超 超 (110)

超 超 超 超 超

冂 口 用 田 里 里 罗 罘 累 累 累 (111)

累 累 累 累 累

| 丨 冂 由 由 由 | | | | | | | | | | | (112) |

| 由 | 由 | 由 | 由 | 由 | | | | | | |

| 丨 冂 日 电 电 | | | | | | | | | | | (113) |

| 电 | 电 | 电 | 电 | 电 | | | | | | |

| 又 又 | | | | | | | | | | | (114) |

| 又 | 又 | 又 | 又 | 又 | | | | | | |

| 厂 厃 反 反 | | | | | | | | | | | (115) |

| 反 | 反 | 反 | 反 | 反 | | | | | | |

| 乀 发 发 发 发 | | | | | | | | | | | (116) |

| 发 | 发 | 发 | 发 | 发 | | | | | | |

| 丶 亠 方 方 放 放 放 放 | | | | | | | | | | | (117) |

| 放 | 放 | 放 | 放 | 放 | | | | | | |

| 丶 亠 六 六 交 交 效 效 效 效 | | | | | | | | | | | (118) |

| 效 | 效 | 效 | 效 | 效 | | | | | | |

# Unit 20

フ 了 己 arr 改 改 改 (119)

改 改 改 改 改

丨 丩 屮 収 收 收 (120)

收 收 收 收 收

丶 丷 丷 广 片 肯 前 前 前 (121)

前 前 前 前 前

亠 亡 立 立 辛 辛 亲 亲 (122)

亲 亲 亲 亲 亲

丿 亻 冂 自 自 自 (123)

自 自 自 自 自

丶 讠 订 订 证 证 证 (124)

证 证 证 证 证

丶 丶 忄 忄 忏 忏 怔 怔 (125)

怔 怔 怔 怔 怔

ノ 彳 彳 彳 行 征 征 征 (126)

征 征 征 征 征

一 丁 丁 下 正 正 正 政 政 政 (127)

政 政 政 政 政

、 广 广 广 疒 疒 疒 疒 症 症 (128)

症 症 症 症 症

6. Making flash cards（做汉字卡片）。

# Unit 21

## I  Old radicals and new characters
### 旧部首和新汉字

心
xīn zì dǐ
心字底

(忄——shù xīnpáng
竖心旁)

heart

- 意: yì 音+心 ▶meaning
  
  \* the real meaning is the sound(音) from one's heart(心)
  
  意思　有意思

- 忘: wàng 亡(sound part)+心 ▶to forget
  
  \* a dead heart cannot remember anything
  
  忘记　忘不了

- 感: gǎn 咸(sound part)+心 ▶to feel
  
  \* someone is moved(心) to tears, and the tear is salty(咸)
  
  感觉　感动

- 忽: hū 勿(sound part)+心 ▶to neglect to; suddenly
  
  \* if you are neglected by someone, you will never(勿) enter into his heart(心)
  
  忽然　忽冷忽热

- 总: zǒng ⺌+口+心 ▶always; to sum up
  
  总是　总和

- 急: jí ⺈+ヨ(sound part)+心 ▶urgent; to worry
  
  \* it is urgent when a knife (⺈) is on your heart
  
  急忙　着急

- 悔: huǐ 忄+每(sound part) ▶to regret
  
  \* somebody feels so regretted about one thing that recall it everyday
  
  后悔　悔改

# Chinese with Me: A Chinese Character Course Book(II)

● 息：自+心　▶breath; to rest
　　xī　zì

\* ancient Chinese people believe that breath comes from heart to nose

气息　休息
　　　　xiū

| jīn |
|---|
| 金(钅) |
| jīn zì páng |
| 金字旁 |
| gold, metal |

● 锻：钅+段(sound part)　▶to forge(iron, etc.)
　　duàn　　duàn

锻炼　锻句

● 销：钅+肖(sound part)　▶to melt
　　xiāo　　xiāo

销路　销售
　　　　shòu

## Exercises 1（练习一）

**1. Choose the correct characters（选择正确的汉字）：**

（1）to forget　　A. 忘　　B. 忙
（2）to feel　　　A. 惑　　B. 感
（3）to neglect　 A. 忽　　B. 忽
（4）urgent　　　A. 急　　B. 息
（5）to melt　　　A. 锁　　B. 销

**2. Reading（读一读，认汉字）：**

意思　什么意思　是什么意思　这句话是什么意思？

忘　忘了　别忘了　别忘了带伞　今天要下雨,别忘了带伞。

感人　很感人　这个故事很感人　你说的这个故事很感人。
　　　　　　　　gù shi　　　　　　　　　　　gù shi

忽冷忽热　为什么忽冷忽热　他为什么对我忽冷忽热的？
　　　　　wèi　　　　　　　wèi

总是　总是很忙　他总是很忙,星期天也不休息。
　　　　　　　　　　　　　　　　　　xiū

急　着急　真着急　钱包没了,真着急。
　　zháo　zhēnzháo　bāo　zhēnzháo

后悔　后悔没有用　现在后悔没有用了　现在后悔有什么用？
hòu　 hòu　yòng　　 hòu　 yòng　　　　　hòu　yòng

休息　好好休息　好好休息吧　你病了就好好休息吧。
xiū　　 xiū　　　 xiū　　　　　　　　　　xiū

锻炼　锻炼的方法　锻炼的方法有很多。

<sup>shòu</sup> <sup>shòuqíngkuàng</sup> <sup>shòuqíngkuàng</sup> <sup>shòuqíngkuàng</sup>
销售　销售情况　销售情况怎么样？　这个月的销售情况怎么样？

# II New radicals and characters
## 新部首和新汉字

**刀(⺈)**
dāo
dāo zì tóu
刀字头
knife

- <sup>dāo</sup> 刀：
  * it is a pictograph of a knife or sword
  小刀　刀子

- <sup>sè</sup>色：⺈+巴 ▶color <sup>bā</sup>
  白色　黑色

- 免：to exempt
  免不了　免费 <sup>fèi</sup>

**目**
mù
mù zì páng
目字旁
eye

- <sup>mù</sup> 目：
  * it is a pictograph of a eye with the eyeball

- 看：手+目 ▶to look after; to look at <sup>kàn shǒu</sup>
  * man raises his hand above his eyes to cut off the sunlight in order to see further and clearly
  看家　看见

- 眠：目+民(sound part) ▶sleep <sup>mián mù mín</sup>
  失眠　冬眠

- 眼：目+艮(sound part) ▶eye <sup>yǎn gěn</sup>
  双眼　眼力

**里**
lǐ
lǐ zì páng
里字旁
inside

- 重/重：千+里 ▶to repeat; heavy <sup>chóng zhòng qiān</sup>
  重现　超重 <sup>chóng zhòng</sup>

## Chinese with Me: A Chinese Character Course Book (II)

- 量/量 : 旦 + 里  ▶ to measure; weight
  - liáng liàng
  - dàn
  - liáng  liàng
  - 量杯  重量

- 后 : after
  - hòu
  - 后天  以后

- 网 : net
  - wǎng
  - \* it is a pictograph of a net
  - 上网  网名

- 无 : no
  - wú
  - 无边  无法

- 业 : course of study
  - yè
  - 行业  学业

## Exercises 2（练习二）

**1. Choose the correct characters（选择正确的汉字）:**

(1) color          A. 包    B. 色
(2) to exempt      A. 免    B. 兔
(3) to look        A. 看    B. 着
(4) heavy          A. 重    B. 量
(5) after          A. 右    B. 后

**2. Reading（读一读，认汉字）:**

白色  喜欢白色  很多人喜欢白色。
（xǐ huan）（xǐ huan）

看  你看  你看这个问题怎么办？

失眠  总是失眠  最近总是失眠  为什么最近总是失眠？
（zuì）（zuì）

眼睛  她的眼睛很大  她的眼睛很大，但是视力不行。
（jīng）（jīng）（jīng）（shì）

重量  箱子的重量  这个箱子重二十公斤。  这个箱子的重量是二十公斤。
（xiāng zi）（xiāng zi）（xiāng zi）

免费  免费上网  可以免费上网  这里可以免费上网吗？
（fèi）（fèi）（fèi）（fèi）

zuò zuò shuì lǎn
以后　工作以后　工作以后,他不能睡懒觉了。

lùn　lùn dào　lùn dào　dōu　xiē
无论　无论走到哪里　无论走到哪里,我都不会忘记你们这些朋友。

zuò　zuò　zuò　zuò　zuòwán
作业　今天的作业　今天的作业很难　今天的作业很难,我还没做完。

## III  Sound parts
## 声旁

肖 to resemble  +  刂  =  削 to cut　　削皮

　　　　　　　+  宀  =  宵 night　　元宵

　　　　　　　+  氵  =  消 to disappear　　消失

　　　　　　　+  雨  =  霄 clouds　　云霄

### Exercises 3（练习三）

1. Combine the radicals and the sound part into characters, then match their English meaning（用所给部首和声旁组成汉字并与英文匹配）:

   宀　　　　　　　clouds
   钅　　　　　　　to melt
   氵　　肖　　　　to disappear
   雨　　　　　　　to cut
   刂　　　　　　　night

2. Please write down other characters with this sound part（用上面的声旁再组几个汉字）:

## IV  Homework
## 课后作业

1. Choose the correct radicals（选择正确的偏旁）：

   （1）wàng (to forget)      A. 忄      B. 心
   （2）huǐ (to regret)       A. 忄      B. 氵
   （3）duàn (to forge)       A. 火      B. 钅
   （4）miǎn (to exempt)      A. 勹      B. 刀
   （5）kàn (to look)         A. 日      B. 目
   （6）xiāo (to disappear)   A. 氵      B. 雨

2. Find the correct pinyin and meaning for the given characters（找找所给汉字正确的拼音和意思）：

   网        色        看        急        眼

   kàn      wǎng      yǎn       sè        jí

3. Circle the phrases with the characters you have learned as many as you can（用所给汉字组成尽可能多的短语）：

   | 意 思 白 感 动 总 |
   | 见 双 色 后 悔 是 |
   | 看 眼 免 失 重 量 |
   | 上 网 无 业 眠 急 |

   1. __意思__    2. _____    3. _____
   4. _____     5. _____    6. _____
   7. _____     8. _____    9. _____
   10. _____    11. _____   12. _____
   13. _____    14. _____   15. _____

4. Read the following paragraph（读一读，认汉字）：

   　　　　　　shāng　zhōumò　jié　dōuyíng　　　　　　　　hòu　　xǐ huan　guàngjiē　mǎi
   　　中国的商店周末和节日都营业，有空的时候，我很喜欢去逛街买东西。
   mǎi　　　　　　　　　　jǐ　　　　　　　　　　　　　　　　　　　　　　　　gé
   买东西还可以锻炼自己的汉语口语和听力。这里的东西价格比较便宜，而
   qiě zhì　　　　　　　　　　　　　jié jì　　　　hòu shāng　cù　　shāngpǐn zhé　　　　　mǎidàogèng
   且质量也不错。过年、过节、换季的时候，商店促销，商品打折，可以买到更

58

便宜的东西。所以我买了很多不太有用的东西。在小商店买东西要讨价还价。开始的时候，我不太习惯。不过，现在已经完全没有问题了。

## 5. Writing (写汉字):

意 — 丶亠土立产音音音意意意意 (129)

忘 — 丶亡亡忘忘忘忘 (130)

感 — 厂厂厂厂厂厂咸咸咸咸感感感 (131)

忽 — 勹勺勿勿忽忽忽忽 (132)

总 — 丶丷丷总总总总总 (133)

急 — 勹夕刍刍急急急急 (134)

悔 — 丶丨忄忄忄忙忙悔悔悔悔 (135)

ノ 亻 自 自 自 自 息 息 息 息 (136)

息 息 息 息 息

丿 卜 卢 卢 车 钅 钅 钅 钅 钅 钅 锻 锻 锻 (137)

锻 锻 锻 锻 锻

丿 卜 卢 卢 车 钅 钅 钅 钅 销 销 销 销 (138)

销 销 销 销 销

刀 刀 (139)

刀 刀 刀 刀 刀

⺈ 夕 久 刍 色 色 (140)

色 色 色 色 色

⺈ 冖 色 臼 兔 兔 兔 (141)

兔 兔 兔 兔 兔

冂 冂 目 目 目 (142)

目 目 目 目 目

# Unit 21

一 二 三 チ チ 矛 看 看 看 看 (143)

看 看 看 看 看

丨 冂 冂 日 日 旷 旷 眠 眠 眠 (144)

眠 眠 眠 眠 眠

丨 冂 冂 日 日 旷 旷 眲 眼 眼 眼 (145)

眼 眼 眼 眼 眼

丨 冂 日 日 甲 甲 里 里 (146)

里 里 里 里 里

一 二 千 千 盲 盲 重 重 重 (147)

重 重 重 重 重

丨 冂 日 旦 早 昌 昌 昌 景 量 量 量 (148)

量 量 量 量 量

丿 厂 厂 斤 后 后 (149)

后 后 后 后 后

冂 冂 冈 冈 网 网 (150)

网 网 网 网 网

一 テ 无 无 (151)

无 无 无 无 无

丨 丨 丷 业 业 业 (152)

业 业 业 业 业

丨 丨 丷 肖 肖 肖 肖 (153)

肖 肖 肖 肖 肖

丨 丨 丷 肖 肖 肖 肖 削 削 (154)

削 削 削 削 削

丶 宀 宀 宀 宀 宵 宵 宵 宵 (155)

宵 宵 宵 宵 宵

丶 氵 氵 氵 汁 汁 消 消 消 消 (156)

消 消 消 消 消

| 一 | 亠 | 一 | 一 | 帀 | 雨 | 雨 | 雷 | 雷 | 雷 | 霄 | 霄 | 霄 | 霄 |
|---|---|---|---|---|---|---|---|---|---|---|---|---|---|
| 霄 | 霄 | 霄 | 霄 | 霄 | | | | | | | | | |

(157)

6. Making flash cards（做汉字卡片）。

# Unit 22

## I Old radicals and new characters
### 旧部首和新汉字

| yán yán |
|:---:|
| 言(讠) |
| yán zì páng |
| 言字旁 |
| word |

- 请:讠+青(sound part)  ▶please
  
  请坐　请问

- 谢:讠+射(身+寸)  ▶to thank
  
  \* we could use three ways to express our thanks:
  
  words(讠), bow(身) or shaking hands(寸)
  
  谢谢　多谢

- 诉:讠+斥  ▶to tell
  
  告诉　诉说

- 讨:讠+寸  ▶to ask for
  
  \* stretching out one's hand (寸) while speaking (讠) to ask for something
  
  讨饭　讨价还价

- 论:讠+仑(sound part)  ▶to discuss
  
  讨论　论文

- 讲:讠+井(sound part)  ▶to tallk
  
  讲话　讲课

- 试:讠+式(sound part)  ▶to try
  
  试一试　试题

- 训:讠+川  ▶to train
  
  训练　培训

64

# Unit 22

| ěr<br>耳<br>ěr zì páng<br>耳字旁<br>ear |

- 聘: 耳+粤(sound part) ▶ to hire (pìn, pīng)
  聘用　聘书

- 职: 耳+只(sound part) ▶ job (zhí, zhī)
  职业　职位

## Exercises 1（练习一）

**1. Choose the correct characters（选择正确的汉字）：**

(1) to tell　　　A. 近　　B. 诉
(2) to discuss　A. 沧　　B. 论
(3) to try　　　A. 试　　B. 诚
(4) to train　　A. 训　　B. 巡
(5) to hire　　　A. 脾　　B. 聘

**2. Reading（读一读，认汉字）：**

请问　请问您为什么来应聘这个职位？

感谢　非常感谢（fēicháng）　非常感谢你们（fēicháng）　非常感谢你们的帮助（fēicháng, bāng）。

告诉（gào）　告诉同学们（gào）告诉同学们明天不上课（gào）　请你告诉同学们明天不上课（gào）。

讨论　讨论一下　再讨论一下　还要再讨论一下　这个问题还要再讨论一下。

试讲　通过试讲　如果通过试讲
　　　如果通过试讲就可以成为我们中心的老师（chéngwéi）。

培训　培训职员（yuán）　培训新职员（yuán）　每年培训新职员（yuán）
　　　我们公司每年培训新职员（yuán）。

招聘　招聘经理（jīng lǐ）　招聘销售部经理（bù jīng lǐ）
　　　那家公司招聘销售部经理（bù jīng lǐ），我想去试试。

# II New radicals and characters
## 新部首和新汉字

| gē<br>戈<br>gē zì páng<br>戈字旁<br>weapon |

- gē<br>戈 : dagger-axe (an ancient weapon)
  * it is a pictograph of an ancient weapon
  dǎo<br>干戈　倒戈

- huò<br>或 : or
  zhě　　xǔ<br>或者　或许

- chéng<br>成 : to become
  　　　wèi<br>成名　成为

- zhàn　　zhàn<br>战 : 占(sound part)＋戈　▶war
  zhēng<br>战争　战场

戈 戈 戈

| lì<br>立<br>lì zì páng<br>立字旁<br>stand |

- lì<br>立 : to stand
  * it is a pictograph of a standing person

- zhàn　　　zhàn<br>站 : 立＋占(sound part)　▶to stand; station
  站起来　车站

- jìng　　xiōng<br>竞 : 立＋兄　▶to compete
  * the competition is even between brothers(兄)
  zhēng<br>竞争　竞走

立 立 立

| zhú<br>竹(⺮)<br>zhú zì tóu<br>竹字头<br>bamboo |

- zhú<br>竹 : bamboo
  * it is a pictograph of two whorls of bamboo leaves

- dá　　　hé<br>答 : ⺮＋合　▶to answer
  　　　àn<br>回答　答案

66

# Unit 22

- 算 (suàn): ⺮ + 目 + 廾　▶ to calculate

  \* it shows two hands (廾) manipulate an abacus (目) made of bamboo (⺮)

  计算 (jì)　算了

- 简 (jiǎn): ⺮ + 间 (jiān) (sound part)　▶ simple

  简单 (dān)　简历 (lì)

- 才 (cái): talent

  人才　天才

- 当 / 当 (dāng/dàng): 丷 + 彐 (jì)　▶ to serve as; when, proper

  当时 (dāng)　适当 (shìdàng)

- 面 (miàn): face

  \* the character is the outline of a face

  当面　面试

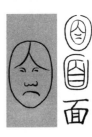

- 就 (jiù): 京 (jīng) + 尤 (yóu) (sound part)　▶ then; just

  就要　就是

## Exercises 2 (练习二)

**1. Choose the correct characters (选择正确的汉字):**

(1) to become　　A. 或　　B. 成

(2) to compete　　A. 竞　　B. 竟

(3) to calculate　　A. 算　　B. 鼻

(4) talent　　　　A. 才　　B. 木

(5) face　　　　　A. 而　　B. 面

**2. Reading (读一读，认汉字):**

或者 (zhě)　星期一或者 (zhě)星期二　星期一或者 (zhě)星期二来

星期一或者 (zhě)星期二来都可以。

战争　没有战争　如果没有战争　如果没有战争该多好啊！
（zhēng）

竞争　竞争的同时
（zhēng）

成为　成为好朋友　在竞争的同时，他们成为了好朋友。
（zhēng）

车站　下一个车站　下一个车站下车　你应该在下一个车站下车。

回答　回答问题　回答这个问题　请你回答这个问题。

简单　太简单了　这道题太简单了　这道题真的太简单了。

算　算错　算错了　你都算错了　连这么简单的题你都算错了。

人才　难得的人才　一个难得的人才　他是一个难得的人才。

方面　哪个方面　哪个方面重要　哪个方面最重要（zuì）

你觉得哪个方面最重要？（zuì）

当　当爸爸　就要当爸爸了　马上就要当爸爸了　他马上就要当爸爸了。

# III  Sound parts
## 声旁

争 to stive （zhēng） + 扌 = 挣 to earn （zhēng）　挣钱

　　　　　　　　　+ 目 = 睁 to open the eyes （zhēng）　睁眼

　　　　　　　　　+ 竹 = 筝 kite （zhēng）　风筝 （fēng）

## Exercises 3 （练习三）

1. Combine the radicals and the sound part into characters, then match their English meaning（用所给部首和声旁组成汉字并与英文匹配）：

竹　　　　　　kite

扌　争　　　　to open the eyes

目　　　　　　to earn

2. Please write down other characters with this sound part（用上面的声旁再组几个汉字）：

_____

# IV Homework
## 课后作业

1. Choose the correct radicals（选择正确的偏旁）：

    （1）qǐng (to please)    A. 讠    B. 氵
    （2）jiǎng (to talk)     A. 亻    B. 讠
    （3）zhí (job)           A. 讠    B. 耳
    （4）zhàn (war)          A. 弋    B. 戈
    （5）zhàn (to stand)     A. 戈    B. 立
    （6）jiǎn (simple)       A. 艹    B. 竹

2. Find the correct pinyin and meaning for the given characters（找找所给汉字正确的拼音和意思）：

    讲            算            战            筝            谢

    suàn         jiǎng         zhàn          xiè          zhēng

3. Circle the phrases with the characters you have learned as many as you can（用所给汉字组成尽可能多的短语）：

    | 成 讨 谢谢 全 面 |
    | 人 才 论 职 当 试 |
    | 战 竞 答 应 聘 简 |
    | 争 回 请 讲 话 便 |

    1. 谢谢      2. _____    3. _____
    4. _____   5. _____    6. _____
    7. _____   8. _____    9. _____
    10. _____   11. _____    12. _____
    13. _____   14. _____    15. _____

## 4. Read the following paragraph (读一读，认汉字):

近几年，上海的经济(jīng jì)发展(zhǎn)得很快。很多外(wài)国和外(wài)地的公司来上海投资(tóu zī)，吸(yǐn)引了很多外(wài)国和外(wài)地的人才来上海找工作。所以，在就业机会增(zēng)加的同时，竞争也变(biàn)得越来越激烈(jī liè)。要想找到一个好工作，学历、外语能力(lì wài néng)、工作经验(jīng)等等都(yàn děng děng dōu)是很重要的条(tiáo)件。找工作的人有不同的要求(qiú)。有的希望(xī wàng)公司就在家的附(fù)近，有的希望到(xī wàng dào)有名的大公司工作，有的希望(xī wàng)工资(zī)高一些(xiē)，有的希望(xī wàng dào)找到轻松(sōng)的工作，还有的希望(xī wàng)工作有挑(tiāo)战。如果你想在上海找工作，你会考虑(kǎo lǜ)哪些(xiē)方面呢？

## 5. Writing (写汉字):

讠 讠 订 计 请 请 请 请 请 请
请 请 请 请 请 (158)

讠 讠 订 讧 讥 询 询 询 谢 谢 谢
谢 谢 谢 谢 谢 (159)

讠 讠 订 诉 诉 诉 诉
诉 诉 诉 诉 诉 (160)

讠 讠 计 讨 讨
讨 讨 讨 讨 讨 (161)

讠 讠 讠 讵 论 论 论
论 论 论 论 论 (162)

# Unit 22

讠 讣 讣 讲 讲 讲 (163)

讲 讲 讲 讲 讲

讠 讠 讠 讠 讠 试 试 试 (164)

试 试 试 试 试

讠 讠 训 训 训 (165)

训 训 训 训 训

丅 丆 千 月 耳 耳 耵 职 聊 聍 聘 聘 (166)

聘 聘 聘 聘 聘

丅 丆 千 月 耳 耳 耵 职 职 职 (167)

职 职 职 职 职

弋 戈 戈 戈 (168)

戈 戈 戈 戈 戈

一 𠃍 丆 亏 弌 或 或 或 (169)

或 或 或 或 或

厂厂厅成成成 (170)

成 成 成 成 成

卜卜占占占战战战 (171)

战 战 战 战 战

丶亠亓立立 (172)

立 立 立 立 立

丶亠亓立立䇂䇂站站站 (173)

站 站 站 站 站

丶亠亓立立音音音竞竞 (174)

竞 竞 竞 竞 竞

丿𠂉𠂉竹竹竹 (175)

竹 竹 竹 竹 竹

丿𠂉𠂉𥫗𥫗𥫗竺竺答答答 (176)

答 答 答 答 答

# Unit 22

⺮ ⺮ ⺮ ⺮ ⺮ 笁 笪 筲 筲 筲 算 算 算 (177)

算 算 算 算 算

⺮ ⺮ ⺮ ⺮ ⺮ 笁 筍 筍 简 简 简 (178)

简 简 简 简 简

丁 才 才 (179)

才 才 才 才 才

丨 ⺌ ⺌ 当 当 当 (180)

当 当 当 当 当

一 丆 丏 而 而 而 面 面 (181)

面 面 面 面 面

丶 亠 亠 亠 古 京 京 㤅 就 就 就 (182)

就 就 就 就 就

⺈ ⺈ 乌 乌 争 争 (183)

争 争 争 争 争

丁 扌 扌 扩 护 抡 抡 挣 挣 (184)

挣 挣 挣 挣 挣

丨 冂 冃 日 日 旷 旷 盺 睁 睁 (185)

睁 睁 睁 睁 睁

丿 ⺮ ⺮ ⺮ ⺮ ⺮ 笁 笁 笁 筝 筝 (186)

筝 筝 筝 筝 筝

6. Making flash cards（做汉字卡片）。

# Unit 23

## I  Old radicals and new characters
### 旧部首和新汉字

| shǒu<br>手<br>shǒu zì páng<br>手字旁<br>(扌—tí shǒupáng 提手旁)<br>hand |
|---|

- 挺：扌+廷(sound part)  ▶rather
  挺好　挺冷

- 报：扌+艮(sound part)  ▶newspaper
  日报　晚报

- 挤：扌+齐(sound part)  ▶crowd; to squeeze
  挤出　挤眼

- 推：扌+隹(sound part)  ▶to push
  推车　推销

- 投：扌+殳(几+又)  ▶to throw
  投放　投诉

- 挑/挑：扌+兆(sound part)  ▶to select; to challenge
  挑选　挑战

- 招：扌+召(sound part, 刀+口)  ▶to beckon
  招手　招聘

- 挂：扌+圭(土+土)  ▶to hang up
  挂号　挂失

- 批：扌+比(sound part)  ▶to criticize
  批文　批评

75

● 拉: 扌 + 立　▶ to pull (lā)
　　拉开　拉面 (lì)

## Exercises 1（练习一）

1. Choose the correct characters（选择正确的汉字）：

　　（1）rather　　　A. 挺　　B. 挺
　　（2）to push　　A. 推　　B. 摊
　　（3）to throw　　A. 投　　B. 技
　　（4）to beckon　A. 抬　　B. 招
　　（5）to hang　　A. 持　　B. 挂

2. Reading（读一读，认汉字）：

挺　挺好的　考得挺好的(kǎo)　大家都考得挺好的(kǎo)。
　　昨天的考试(kǎo)大家都考得挺好的(kǎo)。

报纸(zhǐ)　看报纸(zhǐ)　一边看报纸(zhǐ)一边喝咖啡。
　　每天早上我一边看报纸(zhǐ)一边喝咖啡。

挤　很挤　公共汽车很挤　上下班(bān)的时候公共汽车很挤。

推　门上写着(zhe)"推"字　银行的门上写着(zhe)"推"字。

投资(zī)　来上海投资(zī)　来上海投资(zī)的人　来上海投资(zī)的人越来越多了。

挑战　有挑战的工作　找一个有挑战的工作　我要找一个有挑战的工作。

招手　跟我招手　那个跟我招手的人　我不认识那个跟我招手的人。

挂着(zhe)　挂着(zhe)画(huà)　挂着(zhe)一张(zhānghuà)画　墙(qiáng)上挂着(zhe)一张(zhānghuà)画。

批准(zhǔn)　已经批准(zhǔn)了　申(shēn)请已经批准(zhǔn)了　你的申(shēn)请已经批准(zhǔn)了。

# II New radicals and characters
## 新部首和新汉字

| zhǐ<br>夂<br>zhǐ zì páng<br>夂字旁<br>stop |
|---|

- 夏 (xià): summer
  夏天　夏日

- 处/处 (chǔ/chù): 夂+卜(sound part) ▶to deal with; place
  处方 (chǔ fāng)　住处 (zhù chù)

- 复 (fù): to repeat
  复习　反复

| yè<br>页<br>yè zì páng<br>页字旁<br>head |
|---|

- 预 (yù): 予(yǔ)(sound part)+页 ▶beforehand
  预习　预报

- 额 (é): 客(kè)(sound part)+页 ▶forehead
  额头　前额

- 顺 (shùn): 川(chuān)+页 ▶smooth
  顺路　顺便

- 入 (rù): to enter
  入口　入门

- 申 (shēn): to apply for; another name of Shanghai
  申请　申城

- 支 (zhī): 十(shí)(sound part)+又 ▶to pay
  支出　开支

- 之 (zhī): of
  百分之一　之后

## Exercises 2（练习二）

1. Choose the correct characters（选择正确的汉字）:

（1）summer　　　　　　A. 夏　　B. 复
（2）place　　　　　　　A. 外　　B. 处
（3）smooth　　　　　　A. 顺　　B. 须
（4）to enter　　　　　　A. 八　　B. 人　　C. 入
（5）another name of SH　A. 田　　B. 由　　C. 申　　D. 电
（6）of　　　　　　　　　A. 乙　　B. 之

2. Reading（读一读，认汉字）:

夏天　上海的夏天　六月到八月是上海的夏天，上海的夏天很热。

好处　骑(qí)自行车的好处　骑(qí)自行车的好处是时间比较自由。

预习　复习　预习和复习　上课以前要预习，上课以后要复习。

额度　透(tòu)支额度　透(tòu)支额度是2000美元　这张(zhāng)卡的透(tòu)支额度是2000美元。

一路顺风　祝(zhù)你一路顺风　一切(qiè)顺利(lì)　祝(zhù)你一切(qiè)顺利(lì)。

收入和支出　每个月的收入和支出　每个月的收入和支出是多少?

申请　申请信用卡　去银行申请信用卡　我想去银行申请一张信用卡。

之前　在吃饭之前　在吃饭之前吃　这种药应该在吃饭之前吃。

# III  Sound parts
# 声旁

旦 dawn + 亻 = 但 but　　但是
　　　(dàn)　　(dàn)

　　　　 + 扌 = 担 to carry　担心
　　　　　　　　(dān)

　　　　 + 月 = 胆 gallbladder　胆小
　　　　　　　　(dǎn)

　　　　 + 疒 = 疸 jaundice　黄疸
　　　　　　　　(dǎn)　　　　(huáng)

Unit 23

**Exercises 3**（练习三）

1. Combine the radicals and the sound part into characters, then match their English meaning（用所给部首和声旁组成汉字并与英文匹配）:

   扌     gallbladder
   月  旦  to carry
   亻     but
   疒     jaundice

2. Please write down other characters with this sound part（用上面的声旁再组几个汉字）:

---

# IV  Homework
## 课后作业

1. Choose the correct radicals（选择正确的偏旁）:

   （1）tuī (to push)   A. 又  B. 扌
   （2）tóu (to throw)  A. 讠  B. 扌
   （3）tiāo (to pick)   A. 扌  B. 木
   （4）fù (to repeat)   A. 夂  B. 攵
   （5）shùn (smooth)  A. 贝  B. 页

2. Find the correct pinyin and meaning for the given characters（找找所给汉字正确的拼音和意思）:

   夏    推    额    投    报

   xià    tóu    bào    tuī    é

# Chinese with Me: A Chinese Character Course Book(II)

**3. Circle the phrases with the characters you have learned as many as you can（用所给汉字组成尽可能多的短语）:**

| 夏 天 报 复 预 额 |
|---|
| 申 支 出 入 习 头 |
| 请 挑 口 挂 号 担 |
| 推 战 招 手 顺 心 |

1. 夏天    2. _____    3. _____
4. _____  5. _____    6. _____
7. _____  8. _____    9. _____
10. _____ 11. _____   12. _____
13. _____ 14. _____   15. _____

**4. Read the following paragraph（读一读，认汉字）:**

上个月，贝西去中国建设银行换钱，顺便申请了一张信用卡。银行的工作人员非常热情。当天晚上，她给李大明打电话，请李大明做她的担保人，李大明同意了。第二天，贝西给了银行她的收入证明、护照复印件和李大明的身份证复印件。一个星期以后，她就接到了信用卡中心打给她的电话，说她的申请已经批准了，一个星期之内会用挂号信的方式寄给她。昨天，她收到了银行寄给她的信用卡。这张信用卡是人民币和美元双币种的，透支额度分别是10000人民币和1250美元。年费是80元人民币，但是一年之内使用三次的话，就可以免年费。有了信用卡，以后买东西就更方便了。

**5. Writing（写汉字）:**

丁 扌 扌 扩 托 拝 拝 挺 挺 挺 (187)

挺 挺 挺 挺 挺

丁 扌 扌 护 护 报 报 (188)

报 报 报 报 报

### Unit 23

丁 扌 扌 扩 扩 拚 挤 挤 挤 (189)

挤 挤 挤 挤 挤

丁 扌 扌 扌 扩 扩 拃 拃 推 推 推 (190)

推 推 推 推 推

丁 扌 扌 扩 投 投 投 (191)

投 投 投 投 投

丁 扌 扌 扌 扎 扎 挑 挑 挑 (192)

挑 挑 挑 挑 挑

丁 扌 扌 扌 招 招 招 招 (193)

招 招 招 招 招

丁 扌 扌 扌 扌 扗 挂 挂 挂 (194)

挂 挂 挂 挂 挂

丁 扌 扌 扌 批 批 批 (195)

批 批 批 批 批

十 扌 扌 扩 扩 拉 拉 拉 (196)

拉 拉 拉 拉 拉

一 丁 丌 币 亓 百 百 頁 夏 夏 (197)

夏 夏 夏 夏 夏

丿 夂 処 处 处 (198)

处 处 处 处 处

丿 亇 亇 𠂉 𠂉 复 复 复 (199)

复 复 复 复 复

一 丆 瓦 页 页 页 (200)

页 页 页 页 页

丶 丷 予 予 予 矛 矛 预 预 预 (201)

预 预 预 预 预

丶 亠 宀 宀 宀 客 客 客 客 客 额 额 额 (202)

额 额 额 额 额

Unit 23

丿 刂 刂⁻ 刂⁻ 刂⁻ 顺 顺 顺
(203)
顺 顺 顺 顺 顺

入 入
(204)
入 入 入 入 入

丨 冂 日 申 申
(205)
申 申 申 申 申

十 亠 支 支
(206)
支 支 支 支 支

丶 之 之
(207)
之 之 之 之 之

丨 冂 日 旦 旦
(208)
旦 旦 旦 旦 旦

丿 亻 们 但 但 但
(209)
但 但 但 但 但

| 十 | 扌 | 扌 | 扌 | 扣 | 扣 | 扣 | 担 | 担 | | | | | |
|---|---|---|---|---|---|---|---|---|---|---|---|---|---|

(210)

| 担 | 担 | 担 | 担 | 担 | | | | | | | | | |
|---|---|---|---|---|---|---|---|---|---|---|---|---|---|

| 丿 | 刀 | 月 | 月 | 肝 | 肝 | 胆 | 胆 | 胆 | | | | | |
|---|---|---|---|---|---|---|---|---|---|---|---|---|---|

(211)

| 胆 | 胆 | 胆 | 胆 | 胆 | | | | | | | | | |
|---|---|---|---|---|---|---|---|---|---|---|---|---|---|

| 丶 | 广 | 广 | 广 | 疒 | 疒 | 疖 | 疸 | 疸 | 疸 | | | | |
|---|---|---|---|---|---|---|---|---|---|---|---|---|---|

(212)

| 疸 | 疸 | 疸 | 疸 | 疸 | | | | | | | | | |
|---|---|---|---|---|---|---|---|---|---|---|---|---|---|

6. Making flash cards（做汉字卡片）。

# Unit 24

## 1  Old radicals and new characters
### 旧部首和新汉字

hé
禾
hé mùpáng
禾木旁
grain

- 租: 禾+且(sound part) ▶to rent
  
  \* it is tax paid for a land
  
  出租　租房

- 秋: 禾+火 ▶autumn
  
  \* the grain (禾) ripens under the fiery heat(火) of the sun
  
  秋天　秋冬

- 稍: 禾+肖(sound part) ▶slightly
  
  \* it is the tip of standing grain
  
  稍稍　稍等

- 私: 禾+厶(sound part) ▶private
  
  \* "厶" looks like one's nose, representing private or personal; grains(禾) was used to pay taxes and the residue was private(厶) property in ancient days
  
  私人　私车

- 稳: 禾+急 ▶stable
  
  \* the life is stable when grains exist
  
  稳定　平稳

- 程: 禾+呈(sound part) ▶schedule
  
  日程　行程

- 季: 禾+子(sound part) ▶season
  
  四季　季节

## Exercises 1（练习一）

1. Choose the correct characters（选择正确的汉字）：

    （1）to rent　　　　A. 租　　　B. 稍
    （2）autumn　　　　A. 秒　　　B. 秋
    （3）private　　　　A. 私　　　B. 和
    （4）stable　　　　 A. 稳　　　B. 穗
    （5）season　　　　A. 李　　　B. 季

2. Reading（读一读，认汉字）：

出租车　坐出租车　坐出租车去公司　昨天早上我是坐出租车去公司的。

秋天　秋天来了　秋天来了，天气冷了。

稍后　稍后再拨（zài bō）　请稍后再拨（zài bō）　您拨的电话已关机，请稍后再拨（zài bō）。

私车　买私车的人　买私车的人越来越多　现在买私车的人越来越多了。

稳定（dìng）　稳定（dìng）的职业　一个稳定（dìng）的职业　教师（jiào）是一个稳定（dìng）的职业。

行程　明天的行程　看一下明天的行程　我想看一下明天的行程。

四季　四个季节（jié）　春（chūn）夏秋冬四个季节（jié）　一年有春（chūn）夏秋冬四个季节（jié）。

# II New radicals and characters
## 新部首和新汉字

**欠** (qiàn)
**欠字旁** (qiàn zì páng)
breath, owe

- 欢(huān)：又+欠 ▶joyful
  欢乐(yòu)　欢快

- 歌(gē)：哥(sound part)+欠 ▶song
  歌手(gē)　歌星

- 次(cì)：冫+欠 ▶times
  上次(bīng)　几次

# Unit 24

- 款：士+示+欠 ▶funds
  
  公款　汇款(huì)

- 欣：斤(sound part)+欠 ▶happy
  
  欢欣　欣赏(shǎng)

fāng  
方  
fāng zì páng  
方字旁  
square

- 旅：方+𠂉+𧘇 ▶to travel
  
  * there has 500 soliders in one "旅" in ancient army, the character just looks like a people standing under the flag
  
  旅程　旅行

- 族：方+𠂉+矢(arrow) ▶native
  
  * its original meaning is arrowhead
  
  家族　种族

jīn  
巾  
jīn zì páng  
巾字旁  
towel

- 师：teacher
  
  师生　工程师

- 常：尚(sound part)+巾 ▶often
  
  常常　不常

- 民：people
  
  人民　民族

## Exercises 2（练习二）

1. Choose the correct characters（选择正确的汉字）:

   （1）joyful　　A. 吹　　B. 欢
   （2）native　　A. 族　　B. 旌
   （3）teacher　　A. 帅　　B. 师
   （4）often　　A. 党　　B. 常
   （5）people　　A. 民　　B. 另

## 2. Reading（读一读，认汉字）：

喜欢　喜欢旅行　喜欢跟朋友一起旅行
（xǐ）（xǐ）（xǐ）

我喜欢跟朋友一起旅行，不喜欢跟旅行团。
（xǐ）（xǐ）

唱歌　唱得怎么样　她唱歌唱得怎么样？　她唱歌唱得很好听。

几次　来过几次　你来过几次中国？　我来过七次中国。

贷款　向银行贷款　向银行贷款买房子　很多年轻人向银行贷款买房子。
（dài）（dài）（dài）（dài）

欣赏　欣赏音乐　他一边喝红酒一边欣赏音乐。
（shǎng）（shǎngyīn yuè）（shǎngyīn yuè）

民族　五十六个民族　有五十六个民族　中国有五十六个民族。

围巾　大围巾　冬天用的大围巾　我想买一条冬天用的大围巾。
（wéi）（wéi）（wéi）（wéi）

老师　老师常常　老师常常问我们　老师常常问我们问题。
（lǎo）（lǎo）（lǎo）（lǎo）

# III  Sound parts
# 声旁

羊 sheep + 讠 = 详 detailed　　详细
(yáng)　　　(xiáng)

+ 氵 = 洋 foreign; ocean　　大西洋
(yáng)

+ 木 = 样 appearance　　样子
(yàng)

+ 气 = 氧 oxygen　　氧气
(yǎng)

+ 疒 = 痒 itch　　手痒
(yǎng)

## Exercises 3 (练习三)

1. Combine the radicals and the sound part into characters, then match their English meaning (用所给部首和声旁组成汉字并与英文匹配):

   疒   appearance
   讠   detailed
   氵  羊 ocean
   木   oxygen
   气   itch

2. Please write down other characters with this sound part (用上面的声旁再组几个汉字):

   _____

# IV Homework
## 课后作业

1. Choose the correct radicals (选择正确的偏旁):

   (1) zū (to rent)  A. 扌 B. 禾
   (2) shāo (slightly) A. 木 B. 禾
   (3) gē (song)  A. 欠 B. 夂
   (4) kuǎn (fund)  A. 文 B. 欠
   (5) lǚ (to travel)  A. 万 B. 方
   (6) cháng (often) A. 巾 B. 贝

2. Find the correct pinyin and meaning for the given characters (找找所给汉字正确的拼音和意思):

   秋   歌   师   羊   欢

   gē   huān   shī   qiū   yáng

3. Circle the phrases with the characters you have learned as many as you can（用所给汉字组成尽可能多的短语）:

| 出 | 款 | 私 | 人 | 民 | 稳 |
| 秋 | 租 | 欢 | 欣 | 不 | 族 |
| 四 | 季 | 稍 | 旅 | 多 | 常 |
| 歌 | 后 | 行 | 程 | 次 | 常 |

1. 出租　　2. _____　　3. _____
4. _____　　5. _____　　6. _____
7. _____　　8. _____　　9. _____
10. _____　　11. _____　　12. _____
13. _____　　14. _____　　15. _____

4. Read the following paragraph（读一读，认汉字）:

来中国以后，我有很多收获。特别是我去了很多有意思的地方。我去北京爬了长城，去甘肃走了丝绸之路，去西安看了兵马俑，还去哈尔滨欣赏了冰灯。这些地方都很有意思，而且都各有各的特色。有时候，我参加旅行团，有时候我跟朋友一起自助游。参加旅行团比较方便，但是导游常常要带我们去商店买东西。不参加旅行团的话，当然就比较自由。除了美丽的风景以外，我还看到了一些中国的少数民族。下个月我打算去海南岛。中国太大了，我还有很多地方没有去过。你呢？

5. Writing（写汉字）:

一 二 千 禾 禾 禾 利 租 租 租 租

租 租 租 租 租　　(213)

一 二 千 禾 禾 禾 禾 秋 秋 秋

秋 秋 秋 秋 秋　　(214)

一 二 千 禾 禾 禾 利 利 利 稍 稍 稍

稍 稍 稍 稍 稍　　(215)

二 千 千 禾 私 私 私 (216)
私 私 私 私 私

二 千 千 禾 禾 私 秆 秆 秆 稳 稳 稳 稳 (217)
稳 稳 稳 稳 稳

二 千 千 禾 禾 利 和 积 积 程 程 程 (218)
程 程 程 程 程

二 千 千 禾 禾 季 季 季 (219)
季 季 季 季 季

𠂉 𠂉 欠 欠 (220)
欠 欠 欠 欠 欠

㇇ 又 𣥂 𣥂 欢 欢 (221)
欢 欢 欢 欢 欢

一 丆 苛 可 哥 哥 哥 哥 哥 歌 歌 歌 (222)
歌 歌 歌 歌 歌

丶 冫 冫 次 次 次 (223)
次 次 次 次 次

十 十 土 丰 寺 寺 幸 夹 耒 款 款 款 (224)

款 款 款 款 款

丿 厂 斤 斤 斤 欣 欣 欣 (225)

欣 欣 欣 欣 欣

丶 亠 方 方 方 方 方 旅 旅 旅 (226)

旅 旅 旅 旅 旅

丶 亠 方 方 方 方 方 方 族 族 族 (227)

族 族 族 族 族

冂 巾 巾 (228)

巾 巾 巾 巾 巾

丿 𠂉 𠂊 师 师 师 (229)

师 师 师 师 师

丨 丷 丷 屮 屮 常 常 常 常 常 常 (230)

常 常 常 常 常

# Unit 24

フ コ ヨ 尸 民 民
民 民 民 民 民 (231)

丷 ⺷ 半 兰 羊 羊
羊 羊 羊 羊 羊 (232)

丶 讠 讠 订 汫 洋 详 详
详 详 详 详 详 (233)

丶 氵 氵 汁 洋 洋 洋 洋
洋 洋 洋 洋 洋 (234)

一 十 才 木 木 木 栏 栏 样 样
样 样 样 样 样 (235)

丿 匕 气 气 气 氧 氧 氧 氧
氧 氧 氧 氧 氧 (236)

丶 广 广 疒 疒 疒 疒 疹 痒 痒
痒 痒 痒 痒 痒 (237)

6. Making flash cards（做汉字卡片）。

93

# Unit 25

## 1 Old radicals and new characters
### 旧部首和新汉字

**mén**
门
**mén zì páng**
门字旁
door

- 闹：门+市 ▶noisy
  nào　　shì
  * how noisy it is when a market opens indoor
  热闹　吵闹

**sī**
丝（纟）
**jiǎo sī páng**
绞丝旁
silk

- 约：纟+勺 ▶appointment
  yuē　　sháo
  约会　预约

- 绝：纟+色 ▶absolutely; to discontinue
  jué　　sè
  绝对　绝食

- 续：纟+卖 ▶to continue
  xù　　mài
  连续　续约

- 线：纟+戋(sound part) ▶thread, line
  xiàn　　jiān
  丝线　热线

- 绸：纟+周(sound part) ▶silk
  chóu　　zhōu
  丝绸　绸布
  　　　 bù

- 细：纟+田 ▶thin
  xì　　tián
  细心　细小

- 结：纟+吉(sound part) ▶knot
  jié　　jí
  结婚　结合
  hūn

- 纱：纟+少(sound part) ▶yarn
  shā　　shǎo
  婚纱　纱窗
  hūn　chuāng

94

## Exercises 1 (练习一)

1. Choose the correct characters (选择正确的汉字):

　(1) noisy　　　　　A. 闸　　B. 闹
　(2) appointment　　A. 纣　　B. 约
　(3) thread　　　　　A. 线　　B. 绒
　(4) thin　　　　　　A. 绅　　B. 细
　(5) knot　　　　　　A. 结　　B. 给

2. Reading (读一读,认汉字):

热闹　这里非常热闹　晚上这里非常热闹
　　　一到晚上这里就非常热闹。
（fēi, fēi, fēi above 非）

约会　跟女朋友约会　不能跟女朋友约会了
　　　今天公司加班不能跟女朋友约会了。
（bān above 班）

绝对　绝对放心　你可以绝对放心　我们公司的产品你可以绝对放心。
（chǎn above 产）

手续　办手续　办完手续　手续都办完了吗?

热线　热线电话　打热线电话　有问题请打我们的热线电话。

丝绸　买一些丝绸　买一些丝绸送给朋友
　　　我要去苏州买一些丝绸送给朋友。
（sū zhōu above 苏州）

详细　详细一点　说得详细一点　请你说得详细一点。

结婚　结过婚　结过两次婚　他结过两次婚。
（hūn above 婚）

婚纱　白色的婚纱　穿着白色的婚纱　新娘穿着白色的婚纱。
（hūn, hūn, hūn, xīnniáng, hūn above 婚, 婚, 婚, 新娘, 婚）

# II  New radicals and characters
## 新部首和新汉字

yì
邑

(阝—右耳朵)
yòu ěr duo
city

● 都/都：者+阝　▶all; capital
　　dū　dōu　zhě

首都　都是
dū　dōu

95

- 那: that
  那个　那是

- 部: 咅+⻏ ▶part
  部分　部位

- 郎: 良(sound part)+⻏ ▶man
  * it used ot be a town name
  新郎　牛郎

**示(礻)**
shì zì páng
示字旁
sacrifice

- 视: 礻+见 ▶to look
  近视　视力

- 社: 礻+土 ▶society
  社会　旅行社

- 福: 礻+畐(sound part) ▶blessing
  福气　福如东海

- 礼: manner
  礼物　婚礼

- 祝: 礻+兄 ▶to wish
  祝福　祝酒

- 书: book
  书本　图书馆

- 喜: happy
  * it shows that the happiness is expressed by striking a drum and singing, and Chinese people stick the double happiness "囍" on doors, windows or furniture when they get married
  喜事　喜欢

- 幸：土+羊　▶lucky

  (xìng)　(tǔ)

  \* somebody believes that owing a land (土) and money (羊) is the happiness

  幸福　幸运

## Exercises 2（练习二）

**1. Choose the correct characters（选择正确的汉字）:**

(1) that　　A. 哪　　B. 那
(2) part　　A. 部　　B. 陪
(3) society　A. 社　　B. 祉
(4) wish　　A. 祝　　B. 视
(5) book　　A. 马　　B. 书

**2. Reading（读一读，认汉字）:**

首都　中国的首都　中国的首都在北京(jīng)　北京(jīng)是中国的首都。

那　那些(xiē)　那些(xiē)书　那些(xiē)书都是给你的。

部分　前半部分　小说的前半部分

小说的前半部分写(xiě)得比后半部分好很多。

新(xīn)郎　新(xīn)郎喝(hē)了很多酒　新(xīn)郎在婚(hūn)礼上喝(hē)了很多酒。

电视　看电视　看了一个下午电视　我昨天看了一个下午电视。

社会　到(dào)社会上锻炼　早点到(dào)社会上锻炼

大学生应该早点到(dào)社会上锻炼锻炼。

祝福　祝福你们　真(zhēn)心地祝福你们　我真(zhēn)心地祝福你们。

婚(hūn)礼　参(cān)加婚(hūn)礼　参(cān)加中国人的婚(hūn)礼　这是我第(dì)一次参(cān)加中国人的婚(hūn)礼。

书　一本(běn)书　最(zuì)喜欢的一本(běn)书　我最(zuì)喜欢的一本(běn)书

这是我最(zuì)喜欢的一本(běn)书。

喜事(shì)　大喜事(shì)　一件(jiàn)大喜事(shì)　人生的一件(jiàn)大喜事(shì)

结婚(hūn)是人生(jiàn shì)的一件大喜事。

幸福　幸福的人　最(zuì)幸福的人　自己(jǐ)是最(zuì)幸福的人

她说自己(jǐ)是最(zuì)幸福的人。

## III  Sound parts
## 声旁

包(bāo) to wrap + 扌 = 抱(bào) to hug　拥抱(yōng)

+ 饣 = 饱(bǎo) full　吃饱

+ 氵 = 泡(pào) bubble　灯泡

+ 火 = 炮(pào) cannon　大炮

+ 雨 = 雹(báo) hail　冰雹

### Exercises 3（练习三）

1. Combine the radicals and the sound part into characters, then match their English meaning（用所给部首和声旁组成汉字并与英文匹配）：

   扌　　　　　　　full
   火　　　　　　　to hug
   氵　　包　　　　cannon
   饣　　　　　　　hail
   雨　　　　　　　bubble

2. Please write down other characters with this sound part（用上面的声旁再组几个汉字）：

# IV Homework
## 课后作业

1. Choose the correct radicals（选择正确的偏旁）：

   （1）nào (noisy)　　　A. 门　　B. 口
   （2）xiàn (thread)　　A. 纟　　B. 钅
   （3）dū (capital)　　 A. 阝　　B. 卩
   （4）fú (blessing)　　A. 巾　　B. 礻
   （5）lǐ (manner)　　　A. 木　　B. 礻
   （6）zhù (to wish)　　A. 礻　　B. 衤

2. Find the correct pinyin and meaning for the given characters（找找所给汉字正确的拼音和意思）：

   包　　　结　　　书　　　抱　　　线

   bào　　shū　　xiàn　　bāo　　jié

3. Circle the phrases with the characters you have learned as many as you can（用所给汉字组成尽可能多的短语）：

   | 电视 幸 续 喜 欢 |
   | 线 祝 福 约 细 纱 |
   | 首 都 会 部 热 闹 |
   | 书 社 礼 炮 门 结 |

   1. 电视　　　2. _____　　　3. _____
   4. _____　　5. _____　　　6. _____
   7. _____　　8. _____　　　9. _____
   10. _____　11. _____　　12. _____
   13. _____　14. _____　　15. _____

4. Read the following paragraph（读一读，认汉字）：

   　　　　zhōumò　　　　　　　cān　　mì　zhāng hūn　　　　hūn
   上个周末，我和先生一起参加了秘书小张的婚礼。婚礼是在一家四星
   jí　　　　　　　jǔ　　　xīnniáng chuānzhe　　　hūn　xīn chuānzhe
   级宾馆二楼的百合厅举行的。新娘穿着白色的婚纱，新郎穿着黑色的西
   fú　　　bàn　fēi piàoliang ànzhào　　　　xíguàn
   服，他们都打扮得非常漂亮。按照中国人的习惯，我们送给他们一个红包，

还和他们一起照了相。婚礼很热闹,大概来了二百个客人。大厅里面摆着二十张桌子,每张桌子中间摆着一束玫瑰花。大厅前面挂着他们的照片,墙上贴着一个很大的红双喜字。我在婚礼上发了言,祝他们生活幸福,白头到老。这是我和先生第一次参加中国人的婚礼,我们都觉得很有意思。

5. Writing (写汉字):

丶 门 门 门 闩 闹 闹 闹  (238)
闹 闹 闹 闹 闹

纟 纟 纟 约 约 约  (239)
约 约 约 约 约

纟 纟 纟 纟 约 纺 绐 绝 绝  (240)
绝 绝 绝 绝 绝

纟 纟 纟 纟 纴 纴 绔 绔 续 续 续  (241)
续 续 续 续 续

纟 纟 纟 纟 线 线 线 线  (242)
线 线 线 线 线

Unit 25

| 纟 | 纟 | 纟 | 纫 | 纫 | 绸 | 绸 | 绸 | 绸 | 绸 | | (243) |

| 绸 | 绸 | 绸 | 绸 | 绸 | | | | | | | |

| 纟 | 纟 | 纟 | 纫 | 纫 | 细 | 细 | 细 | | | | (244) |

| 细 | 细 | 细 | 细 | 细 | | | | | | | |

| 纟 | 纟 | 纟 | 纣 | 纣 | 纣 | 结 | 结 | 结 | | | (245) |

| 结 | 结 | 结 | 结 | 结 | | | | | | | |

| 纟 | 纟 | 纟 | 纫 | 纱 | 纱 | 纱 | | | | | (246) |

| 纱 | 纱 | 纱 | 纱 | 纱 | | | | | | | |

| 冂 | 口 | 吕 | 吕 | 吕 | 邑 | 邑 | | | | | (247) |

| 邑 | 邑 | 邑 | 邑 | 邑 | | | | | | | |

| 十 | 土 | 耂 | 才 | 者 | 者 | 者 | 者 | 都 | 都 | | (248) |

| 都 | 都 | 都 | 都 | 都 | | | | | | | |

| 刁 | 刁 | 月 | 那 | 那 | 那 | | | | | | (249) |

| 那 | 那 | 那 | 那 | 那 | | | | | | | |

亠 亠 六 立 产 咅 音 音 部 部 部 (250)

部 部 部 部 部

乛 ㇇ 彐 㠯 㠯 郎 郎 郎 (251)

郎 郎 郎 郎 郎

一 亍 亍 示 示 (252)

示 示 示 示 示

丶 ㇇ ㇇ 礻 礻 视 视 视 视 (253)

视 视 视 视 视

丶 ㇇ ㇇ 礻 礻 社 社 社 (254)

社 社 社 社 社

丶 ㇇ ㇇ 礻 礻 衤 衤 衤 福 福 福 福 福 (255)

福 福 福 福 福

丶 ㇇ ㇇ 礻 礼 礼 (256)

礼 礼 礼 礼 礼

# Unit 25

丶 亅 礻 礻 礻 祀 祀 祝 祝 (257)

祝 祝 祝 祝 祝

フ 书 书 书 (258)

书 书 书 书 书

十 士 吉 吉 吉 吉 吉 壴 壴 喜 喜 喜 (259)

喜 喜 喜 喜 喜

十 士 士 吉 吉 幸 幸 幸 (260)

幸 幸 幸 幸 幸

勹 勺 匀 包 包 (261)

包 包 包 包 包

十 才 才 扌 扚 扚 抱 抱 (262)

抱 抱 抱 抱 抱

丿 ⺈ 乍 饣 饣 饣 饱 饱 (263)

饱 饱 饱 饱 饱

丶 氵 氵 汋 沟 泡 泡 泡 (264)

泡 泡 泡 泡 泡

丶 丷 ⺀ 灬 灯 灯 炮 炮 炮 (265)

炮 炮 炮 炮 炮

一 厂 币 币 雨 雨 雨 雪 雪 雷 雷 电 (266)

电 电 电 电 电

6. Making flash cards (做汉字卡片)。

# Unit 26

## I  Old radicals and new characters
### 旧部首和新汉字

| 口 |
|---|
| guó zìkuāng |
| 国字框 |
| enclose |

- 团 : 口 + 才 (tuán / cái) ▶ group
  
  团结　旅行团

- 围 : 口 + 韦 (sound part) (wéi / wéi) ▶ group
  
  围巾　包围

| 宀 |
|---|
| bǎo gài tóu |
| 宝盖头 |
| home |

- 容 : 宀 + 谷 (róng / gǔ) ▶ to hold
  
  \* both home(宀) and valley(谷) can hold people or things
  
  容量　包容

- 安 : 宀 + 女 (ān / nǚ) ▶ safe
  
  \* man thinks that to attain peace or safe he should confine his woman within the house
  
  安全　安心

- 完 : 宀 + 元 (sound part) (wán / yuán) ▶ to complete
  
  完成　看完

- 定 (dìng) : stable
  
  一定　稳定

- 客 : 宀 + 各 (sound part) (kè / gè) ▶ guest
  
  客人　客厅

- 宿 : 宀 + 亻 + 百 (sù / bǎi) ▶ dormitory
  
  \* a hundred of people living under one roof is a dormitory
  
  住宿　宿舍 (shě)

105

- 实:<sup>shí</sup> 宀+头<sup>tóu</sup>  ▶true
  
  实用　实力

## Exercises 1（练习一）

1. Choose the correct characters:

   （1）group　　　　A. 团　　B. 困
   （2）to surround　　A. 围　　B. 国
   （3）complete　　　A. 完　　B. 宗
   （4）guest　　　　 A. 容　　B. 客
   （5）true　　　　　A. 买　　B. 实

2. Reading（读一读，认汉字）：

   旅行团　跟旅行团　不跟旅行团　这次旅行我们不跟旅行团。

   围　围了那么多人　怎么围了那么多人　那边怎么围了那么多人？

   容易　容易感冒　这样的天气很容易感冒。

   平安　平平安安　平平安安回家　高高兴兴上班，平平安安回家。

   完　上完课　一上完课　我一上完课　我一上完课就去你家。

   一定　不一定　明天他一定会来　明天他一定不会来　明天他不一定会来。

   客人　五十位客人　请了五十位客人　我请了五十位客人来参加晚会。

   住宿　住宿费　宿舍的住宿费　学校宿舍的住宿费不算高。

   实在　实在没有时间　我实在没有时间去旅行。

# II New radicals and characters
## 新部首和新汉字

草(艹)
cǎo zì tóu
草字头
plant

- 花: 艹+化(sound part)  ▶flower
  
  开花　花心

# Unit 26

- <sup>yào</sup>药: ⺾ + 约<sup>yuē</sup>  ▶medicine

  * it implies herbs (⺾) can restrain (约) sickness

  吃药　中药

- <sup>jié</sup>节: ⺾ + 卩<sup>dān</sup>  ▶section; festival

  关节　节日

- <sup>yíng</sup>营: camp

  * go to camp on a grassland (⺾)

  营地　营业

- <sup>huò</sup>获: ⺾ + 犭 + 犬<sup>quǎn</sup>  ▶to gain (犬)

  * with a dog's (犬) help, a hunter gains an animal (犭) on a grassland (⺾)

  获得　获取

- <sup>chá</sup>茶: tea

  红茶　茶杯

| 衣(衤) |
|---|
| yī zì páng |
| 衣字旁 |
| clothes |

- <sup>biǎo</sup>表: surface

  * it refers to the surface of the clothes

  表面　表现

- <sup>chū</sup>初: 衤 + 刀<sup>dāo</sup>  ▶beginning

  * begin to make clothes (衤) by using scissors (刀)

  年初　起初

- <sup>chèn</sup>衬: 衤 + 寸<sup>cùn</sup> (sound part)  ▶shirt

  衬衣　衬托<sup>tuō</sup>

- <sup>shān</sup>衫: 衤 + 彡<sup>sān</sup> (sound part)  ▶shirt

  衬衫　运动衫

- <sup>yòng</sup>用: to use

  不用　用法

- 习 <sup>xí</sup> : to study

*it is a pictograph of bird's wing, suggesting a young bird learning to fly

学习    见习

## Exercises 2 (练习二)

**1. Choose the correct characters (选择正确的汉字):**

(1) camp　　　A. 营　　B. 菅
(3) tea　　　　A. 茶　　B. 荼
(3) surface　　A. 表　　B. 裴
(4) to use　　　A. 用　　B. 甩
(5) to study　　A. 刁　　B. 习

**2. Reading (读一读, 认汉字):**

花　买花　节日里买花　节日里买花很贵(guì)。

中药　试试中药吧　西药没有用,试试中药吧。

节日　最(zuì)热闹的节日　最(zuì)大最(zuì)热闹的节日　春节是中国最(zuì)大最(zuì)热闹的节日。

营业　营业时间　那家商店(shāng)的营业时间　你知道那家商店(shāng)的营业时间吗?

获得　获得了第(dì)一名　他获得了运动会跑步比赛(sài)的第(dì)一名。

茶　喝(hē)茶　喝(hē)茶有好处　喝(hē)茶很有好处　喝(hē)茶对身体很有好处。

表示　表示感谢　向(xiàng)他表示感谢　我给他写信向(xiàng)他表示感谢。

初一　年初一　年初一要去父母家　年初一要去父母家给他们拜(bài)年。

衬衫　丝绸衬衫　穿(chuān)丝绸衬衫　喜欢穿(chuān)丝绸衬衫

夏天我喜欢穿(chuān)丝绸衬衫。

用　用筷(kuài)子　用筷(kuài)子吃饭　不会用筷(kuài)子吃饭　我还不会用筷(kuài)子吃饭呢。

学习　好好学习　好好学习,天天向上。

## III  Sound parts
## 声旁

风 wind + 讠 = 讽 (fēng) to mock (cì) 讽刺

+ 木 = 枫 (fēng) maple (yè) 枫叶

+ 疒 = 疯 (fēng) crazy 发疯

### Exercises 3（练习三）

1. Combine the radicals and the sound part into characters, then match their English meaning（用所给部首和声旁组成汉字并与英文匹配）:

   疒            crazy
   讠    风     maple
   木            to mock

2. Please write down other characters with this sound part（用上面的声旁再组几个汉字）:

---

## IV  Homework
## 课后作业

1. Choose the correct radicals（选择正确的偏旁）:

   （1）tuán (group)        A. 门      B. 囗
   （2）róng (to hold)      A. 宀      B. 穴
   （3）sù (dormitory)      A. 冖      B. 宀
   （4）huā (flower)        A. 艹      B. 衤
   （5）chū (beginning)     A. 礻      B. 衤
   （6）shān (shirt)        A. 木      B. 衤

2. Find the correct pinyin and meaning for the given characters（找找所给汉字正确的拼音和意思）：

花　　　　　风　　　　　药　　　　　茶　　　　　枫

　fēng　　　　　huā　　　　　fēng　　　　　chá　　　　　yào

3. Circle the phrases with the characters you have learned as many as you can（用所给汉字组成尽可能多的短语）：

衬衫 包 获 习 药
团 结 围 安 得 用
请 实 节 约 定 完
客 风 力 花 茶 成

1. 衬衫　　2. _____　　3. _____
4. _____　　5. _____　　6. _____
7. _____　　8. _____　　9. _____
10. _____　　11. _____　　12. _____
13. _____　　14. _____　　15. _____

4. Read the following paragraph（读一读，认汉字）：

　　中国人和世界上所有国家的人一样都喜欢收到礼物。中国人在收到礼物后一般不马上打开看，而是等客人走了以后再打开。这是尊重送礼物的人的表现。因为中国人觉得送什么礼物不重要，重要的是朋友之间的友谊。有些国家的习惯跟中国不一样。收到礼物后会马上打开看，还要称赞礼物，表示感谢，这也是尊重送礼物的人的表现。所以，在不同的国家，或者对不同国家的人，最好按照当地的习惯去做。

5. Writing（写汉字）：

丨 冂 冂 用 用 团 团

(267)

团 团 团 团 团

## Unit 26

冂 门 冂 同 闱 围 围 (268)
围 围 围 围 围

丶 宀 宀 宀 宀 突 突 容 容 容 (269)
容 容 容 容 容

丶 宀 宀 安 安 安 (270)
安 安 安 安 安

丶 宀 宀 宀 宀 完 完 (271)
完 完 完 完 完

丶 宀 宀 宀 宀 宅 定 定 (272)
定 定 定 定 定

丶 宀 宀 宀 安 安 客 客 客 (273)
客 客 客 客 客

丶 宀 宀 宀 宀 宁 宿 宿 宿 宿 (274)
宿 宿 宿 宿 宿

丶 宀 宀 宀 宇 实 实 实 (275)
实 实 实 实 实

一 艹 艹 艹 艹 苢 苩 草 草 (276)
草 草 草 草 草

一 艹 艹 艹 花 花 花 (277)
花 花 花 花 花

一 艹 艹 艹 艼 芗 药 药 药 (278)
药 药 药 药 药

一 艹 艹 节 节 (279)
节 节 节 节 节

一 艹 艹 艹 芦 带 带 营 营 营 (280)
营 营 营 营 营

一 艹 艹 艹 狄 荻 获 获 获 (281)
获 获 获 获 获

一 十 艹 艾 芯 芩 芩 茶 茶 (282)

茶 茶 茶 茶 茶

一 亠 ナ 衣 衣 衣 (283)

衣 衣 衣 衣 衣

一 二 丰 丰 丰 表 表 表 (284)

表 表 表 表 表

ㄧ ㄜ ㄤ ㄤ 衤 初 初 (285)

初 初 初 初 初

ㄧ ㄜ ㄤ ㄤ 衤 衤 衬 衬 (286)

衬 衬 衬 衬 衬

ㄧ ㄜ ㄤ ㄤ 衤 衤 衫 衫 衫 (287)

衫 衫 衫 衫 衫

𠃍 ⺆ 月 用 用 (288)

用 用 用 用 用

6. Making flash cards (做汉字卡片)。

# Unit 27

## I  Old radicals and new characters
### 旧部首和新汉字

| chǎng |
|---|
| 厂 |
| chǎngzì páng |
| 厂字旁 |
| factory |

- 历(lì)：厂+力(lì)(sound part) ▶experience
  历史(chǎng)  挂历(lì)

- 原(yuán)：厂+白(bái)+小(xiǎo) ▶original
  原来  原本

- 厉(lì)：厂+万(wàn) ▶severe
  严厉(yán)  厉害(hài)

| yuè |
|---|
| 月 |
| yuè zì páng |
| 月字旁 |
| moon / meat |

- 脸(liǎn)：月+佥(qiān)(sound part) ▶face
  洗脸  脸红

- 肯(kěn)：止(zhǐ)+月 ▶to be willing to
  不肯  肯定

- 能(néng)：can
  全能  能力

- 服(fú)：clothes
  衣服  西服

- 脑(nǎo)：brain
  大脑  电脑

115

Chinese with Me: A Chinese Character Course Book(II)

**Exercises 1**（练习一）

1. Choose the correct characters（选择正确的汉字）:

   （1）experience　　　　A. 历　　B. 厉
   （2）original　　　　　A. 原　　B. 厡
   （3）to be willing to　A. 背　　B. 肯
   （4）can　　　　　　　A. 脂　　B. 能
   （5）brain　　　　　　A. 脑　　B. 胸

2. Reading（读一读,认汉字）:

   经历　人生经历　有意思的人生经历　在中国的生活是很有意思的人生经历。

   原来　原来你就是小王的哥哥。

   　　　　hài　　　　hài　　　　　　hài
   厉害　太厉害了　她太厉害了,会说五种语言。

   　　　　　　　　hē　　　　　　hē
   脸　脸红　喝酒脸红　我一喝酒脸就红。

   肯定　肯定回家　肯定回家过年　我答应了父母今年肯定回家过年。

   　　　　　　sheng　　　　　　　　sheng
   不能　不能大声说话　图书馆里不能大声说话。

   衣服　这件衣服　这件衣服没洗干净。

   　　　　　　jiāo　　　　　　jiāo　　　　　　　jiāo
   电脑　用电脑　教妈妈用电脑　我教妈妈用电脑　妈妈要我教她用电脑。

# II  New radicals and characters
## 新部首和新汉字

| 刂 |
|---|
| lì dāopáng |
| 立刀旁 |
| knife |

- 到：至+刂　▶to arrive
  来到　到站

- 别：另+刂　▶other
  别的　别人

- 副：畐(sound part)+刂　▶other
  一副　全副

116

# Unit 27

- 剧：居(sound part)＋刂 ▶drama
  
  电视剧　剧本

- 利：禾＋刂 ▶sharp; benefit
  
  \* the knife should be sharp for reaping the grain
  
  有利　利息

yù　wáng
**玉(王)**
yù zì páng
玉字旁
jade

- 班：王＋刂＋王 ▶class
  
  \* using a knife to divide a gem equally, now it means people are divided into different classes
  
  同班　加班

- 理：王＋里(sound part, 田＋土) ▶reason
  
  \* either the cutting of a gem or the dividing of field(田) and land(土) needs to be reasonable
  
  理由　原理

- 环：王＋不 ▶circle
  
  耳环　连环

- 球：王＋求(sound part) ▶ball
  
  足球　环球

- 丰：rich
  
  丰收　丰富

- 乐/樂：happy; music
  
  可乐　乐队

## Exercises 2（练习二）

1. Choose the correct characters（选择正确的汉字）:

   (1) drama　　　A. 剧　　B. 刷
   (2) sharp　　　A. 刊　　B. 利
   (3) class　　　A. 珏　　B. 班
   (4) circle　　　A. 坏　　B. 环
   (5) happy　　　A. 乐　　B. 东

117

## 2. Reading（读一读，认汉字）：

到家　到家以后　我到家以后给你打电话。

别的　别的地方　到别的地方去　我想再到别的地方去看看。
　　　　　　　　　　　　　　　　zài

一副耳环　一副手套　一副眼镜
　　tào　　　　jìng

京剧　听不懂京剧　中国人听不懂京剧　连中国人也听不懂京剧。
　　　　dǒng　　　　　dǒng　　　　　　　dǒng

利用　利用机会　利用这个机会　你要利用这个机会好好学习。

我们班　我们班一共有二十八个学生。
　　　　　　gòng

管理　管理好公司　管理好这么大的公司　管理好这么大的公司很难。
guǎn　guǎn　　　　guǎn　　　　　　　　guǎn

环球　环球旅行　做一次环球旅行　我的梦想是做一次环球旅行。
　　　　　　　　　　　　　　　　mèng

丰富　丰富多了　现在的生活丰富多了　现在的生活比过去丰富多了。
fù　　fù　　　　　　fù　　　　　　　　　　fù

音乐　快乐　听音乐　听音乐能使人快乐。
　　　　　　　　　　　　shǐ

# III　Sound parts
## 声旁

专 expert ＋ 亻 ＝ 传 to transfer　　传送
zhuān　　　　　　chuán

　　　　　　　　传 biography　　自传
　　　　　　　　zhuàn

＋ 车 ＝ 转 to turn　　左转
　　　　zhuǎn

　　　　转 to revolve　　自转
　　　　zhuàn

＋ 石 ＝ 砖 brick　　砖头
　　　　zhuān

## Exercises 3（练习三）

1. Combine the radicals and the sound part into characters, then match their English meaning（用所给部首和声旁组成汉字并与英文匹配）：

    石　　　　　　to turn
    　　　　　　　to transfer
    亻　　专　　　brick
    车　　　　　　to revolve
    　　　　　　　biography

2. Please write down other characters with this sound part（用上面的声旁再组几个汉字）：

_____

# IV Homework
## 课后作业

1. Choose the correct radicals（选择正确的偏旁）：

    （1）lì (experience)　　A. 厂　　B. 厂
    （2）yuán (original)　　A. 厂　　B. 乁
    （3）lì (severe)　　　　A. 厂　　B. 广
    （4）liǎn (face)　　　　A. 日　　B. 月
    （5）fú (clothes)　　　A. 月　　B. 礻
    （6）lǐ (reason)　　　　A. 土　　B. 王

2. Find the correct pinyin and meaning for the given characters（找找所给汉字正确的拼音和意思）：

    脑　　　　脸　　　　服　　　　转　　　　砖

    liǎn　　　fú　　　　nǎo　　　zhuàn　　zhuān

3. Circle the phrases with the characters you have learned as many as you can (用所给汉字组成尽可能多的短语):

| 剧 原 来 历 肯 定 |
|---|
| 副 本 理 到 别 人 |
| 班 能 丰 脸 电 脑 |
| 乐 专 利 息 服 气 |

1. 原来　　2. _____　　3. _____
4. _____　5. _____　　6. _____
7. _____　8. _____　　9. _____
10. _____　11. _____　12. _____
13. _____　14. _____　15. _____

4. Read the following paragraph (读一读, 认汉字):

现在我们每周休息两天，周末的时间比过去长了，生活也更丰富了。有的喜欢和全家团聚，大家一起做一些好吃的饭菜，聊聊一周的新闻；有的喜欢约朋友出去玩，逛逛街、唱唱歌、跳跳舞、看看电影什么的；还有的去学校学习外语、电脑、管理等专业知识和技术。为了培养孩子，有些父母不得不利用周末带孩子去各种辅导班学习。我呢，最喜欢睡懒觉，想睡到几点就睡到几点。你一般怎么过周末呢？

5. Writing (写汉字):

厂厅历历　(294)
历 历 历 历 历

厂厂厂厂历历原原原原　(295)
原 原 原 原 原

# Unit 27

厂 厂 厅 厉 厉
(296)

厉 厉 厉 厉 厉

丿 几 月 月 朋 朎 朎 脸 脸 脸
(297)

脸 脸 脸 脸 脸

丨 卜 止 止 肯 肯 肯 肯
(298)

肯 肯 肯 肯 肯

厶 仏 台 台 台 台 能 能 能
(299)

能 能 能 能 能

丿 几 月 月 朋 服 服 服
(300)

服 服 服 服 服

丿 几 月 月 朋 朎 朓 脑 脑 脑
(301)

脑 脑 脑 脑 脑

一 丆 云 至 至 到 到 到
(302)

到 到 到 到 到

121

| 丨 口 ㅁ 另 别 别 别 | | | | | | | | | |
|---|---|---|---|---|---|---|---|---|---|
| 别 | 别 | 别 | 别 | 别 | | | | | |

(303)

| 一 ㄧ 亓 戸 亯 亯 咼 畐 副 副 | | | | | | | | | |
|---|---|---|---|---|---|---|---|---|---|
| 副 | 副 | 副 | 副 | 副 | | | | | |

(304)

| 一 尸 尸 尸 居 居 居 剧 剧 | | | | | | | | | |
|---|---|---|---|---|---|---|---|---|---|
| 剧 | 剧 | 剧 | 剧 | 剧 | | | | | |

(305)

| 一 千 千 禾 禾 利 利 | | | | | | | | | |
|---|---|---|---|---|---|---|---|---|---|
| 利 | 利 | 利 | 利 | 利 | | | | | |

(306)

| 一 干 王 玉 玉 | | | | | | | | | |
|---|---|---|---|---|---|---|---|---|---|
| 玉 | 玉 | 玉 | 玉 | 玉 | | | | | |

(307)

| 一 干 王 玉 玗 玗 玨 班 班 班 | | | | | | | | | |
|---|---|---|---|---|---|---|---|---|---|
| 班 | 班 | 班 | 班 | 班 | | | | | |

(308)

| 一 干 王 玉 玗 玗 玾 理 理 理 理 | | | | | | | | | |
|---|---|---|---|---|---|---|---|---|---|
| 理 | 理 | 理 | 理 | 理 | | | | | |

(309)

# Unit 27

二 𠄠 𡉄 王 王 玡 环 环 (310)

环 环 环 环 环

二 𠄠 𡉄 王 王 玡 玠 玮 玮 球 球 球 (311)

球 球 球 球 球

一 二 三 丰 (312)

丰 丰 丰 丰 丰

一 厂 斤 乐 乐 (313)

乐 乐 乐 乐 乐

一 二 专 专 (314)

专 专 专 专 专

亻 亻 仁 传 传 传 (315)

传 传 传 传 传

一 𠃌 车 车 车 车 转 转 转 (316)

转 转 转 转 转

| 丁 | 丆 | 不 | 石 | 石 | 石 | 砖 | 砖 | 砖 | | | |
|---|---|---|---|---|---|---|---|---|---|---|---|

(317)

| 砖 | 砖 | 砖 | 砖 | 砖 | | | | | | | |
|---|---|---|---|---|---|---|---|---|---|---|---|

6. Making flash cards (做汉字卡片)。

# Unit 28

## 1 Old radicals and new characters
### 旧部首和新汉字

| tǔ |
|---|
| 土 |
| tǔ zì páng |
| 土字旁 |
| earth, land |

- 堵(dǔ)：土＋者(zhě) ▶block

  堵车　堵心

- 均(jūn)：土＋匀(yún)(sound part) ▶equal

  平均　均分

- 址(zhǐ)：土＋止(zhǐ)(sound part) ▶site

  地址　住址

- 型(xíng)：刑(xíng)(sound part)＋土 ▶model

  型号　脸型

- 培(péi)：土＋音(pǒu) ▶to foster

  培训　培养

- 增(zēng)：土＋曾(céng)(sound part) ▶to add

  增加　增高

- 圣(shèng)：又(yòu)＋土 ▶holy

  圣人　神圣

- 坏(huài)：土＋不(bù) ▶bad

  好坏　坏处

## Exercises 1（练习一）

1. Choose the correct characters（选择正确的汉字）:

   （1）equal　　A. 均　　B. 均

   （2）site　　　A. 地　　B. 址

125

(3) model     A. 坚     B. 型

(4) to add     A. 增     B. 增

(5) bad     A. 坏     B. 坏

2. Reading（读一读，认汉字）：

堵车　因为堵车　因为堵车，今天我又迟到了。

平均　平均寿命（shòumìng）　中国女性（xìng）的平均寿命（shòumìng）

中国女性（xìng）的平均寿命（shòumìng）是80岁（suì）。

地址　你的地址　写（xiě）一下你的地址　请在这里写（xiě）一下你的地址。

型号　最新（zuì xīn）型号　刚刚（gānggāng）推出的最新（zuì xīn）型号

这是公司刚刚（gānggāng）推出的最新（zuì xīn）型号。

培养（yǎng）　培养（yǎng）成才　把孩（hái）子培养（yǎng）成才　父母都想把孩（hái）子培养（yǎng）成才。

增加　房租增加了　房租又增加了　这个月的房租又增加了。

圣诞（dàn）节　圣诞（dàn）节很重要　对很多国家的人来说圣诞（dàn）节很重要。

坏　我的自行车坏了　我的自行车坏了，你会修（xiū）吗？

## II  New radicals and characters
### 新部首和新汉字

**贝** (bèi)
贝字旁 (bèi zì páng)
treasure

- 费 (fèi)：弗(fú)+贝 ▶fee
  费用　学费

- 质 (zhì)：quality
  质量　质地

- 资 (zī)：次(cì)(sound part)+贝 ▶fund
  资金　资本

## Unit 28

- 赏 (shǎng/shàng)：尚 (sound part)+贝 ▶to enjoy
  赏月　欣赏

- 贴 (tiē)：贝+占 (zhàn) ▶to stick
  贴身　贴近

- 赞 (zàn)：先+先 (xiān, sound part)+贝 (xiān) ▶to praise
  赞美 (měi)　赞赏

- 赔 (péi)：贝+咅 (pǒu) ▶to compensate
  赔本　理赔

**石** (shí)
**石字旁** (shí zì páng)
stone

- 码 (mǎ)：石+马 (mǎ, sound part) ▶code
  号码　密码 (mì)

- 碎 (suì)：石+卒 (zú) ▶broken
  心碎　粉碎

- 破 (pò)：石+皮 (pí) ▶broken
  破碎　破坏

- 沪 (hù)：氵+户 (hù, sound part) ▶abbreviation of Shanghai

- 单 (dān)：single
  单人　单身

## Exercises 2（练习二）

1. Choose the correct characters（选择正确的汉字）:

   (1) treasure　　A. 贝　　B. 见
   (2) fee　　　　A. 贵　　B. 费
   (3) fund　　　 A. 贤　　B. 资
   (4) to stick　　A. 贴　　B. 赔
   (5) single　　　A. 卑　　B. 单　　C. 单

## 2. Reading (读一读，认汉字)：

学费　学费很贵(guì)　上大学学费很贵(guì)　去外(wài)国上大学学费很贵(guì)吧？

质量　看重质量　我最(zuì)看重质量　买东西的时候(hou)我最(zuì)看重质量。

资金　大量的资金　需(xū)要大量的资金　这个项(xiàng)目需(xū)要大量的资金。

赏月　一起赏月　全家一起赏月　中秋节的晚上全家一起赏月。

贴着(zhe)　贴着(zhe)一张(zhāng)中国地(tú)图　教(jiào)室的墙(qiáng)上贴着(zhe)一张(zhāng)中国地(tú)图。

称(chēng)赞　被(bèi)别人称(chēng)赞　中国人被(bèi)别人称(chēng)赞的时候(hou)说：哪里哪里。

赔款　得到赔款　得不到赔款　我为什么得不到赔款？

号码　电话号码　你的电话号码　能告(gào)诉我你的电话号码吗？

打碎　被(bèi)我打碎了　花瓶(píng bèi)被我打碎了　妈妈最(zuì)喜欢的花瓶(píng bèi)被我打碎了。

切(qiē)破　被(bèi)刀切(qiē)破了　手指(zhǐ bèi)被刀切(qiē)破了　我的手指(zhǐ bèi)被菜刀切(qiē)破了。

沪　沪是上海的简称(chēng)　上海简称(chēng)沪。

单身　还是单身　现在还是单身　到现在还是单身　他到现在还是单身。

# III Sound parts
# 声旁

马(mǎ) horse + 女 = 妈(mā) mum　妈妈

　　　　+ 王 = 玛(mǎ) agate　玛瑙(nǎo)

　　　　+ 叩(xuān) = 骂(mà) to curse　打骂

　　　　+ 虫(chóng) = 蚂(mǎ) ant　蚂蚁(yǐ)

## Exercises 3（练习三）

1. Combine the radicals and the sound part into characters, then match their English meaning（用所给部首和声旁组成汉字并与英文匹配）：

   虫              agate
   口              ant
   叩    马       measure word
   王              to curse
   女              mum
   石              code

2. Please write down other characters with this sound part（用上面的声旁再组几个汉字）：

_____

# IV Homework
## 课后作业

1. Choose the correct radicals（选择正确的偏旁）：

   （1）shèng (holy)           A. 工   B. 土
   （2）huài (bad)             A. 土   B. 木
   （3）shǎng (to enjoy)       A. 贝   B. 见
   （4）péi (to compensate)    A. 土   B. 贝
   （5）pò (broken)            A. 土   B. 石
   （6）hù (Shanghai)          A. 氵   B. 火

2. Find the correct pinyin and meaning for the given characters（找找所给汉字正确的拼音和意思）：

   妈          型          堵          蚂          费

   dǔ          mǎ          fèi         mā          xíng

3. Circle the phrases with the characters you have learned as many as you can（用所给汉字组成尽可能多的短语）:

| 堵 地 址 培 欣 增 |
| 坏 车 费 均 赏 破 |
| 贴 型 号 码 赔 碎 |
| 沪 单 投 资 金 款 |

1. 地址　　　2. _____　　　3. _____
4. _____　　5. _____　　　6. _____
7. _____　　8. _____　　　9. _____
10. _____　　11. _____　　12. _____
13. _____　　14. _____　　15. _____

4. Read the following paragraph（读一读，认汉字）:

马克原来打算上个月离开中国，但是由于工作原因，他不得不推迟了几个星期。昨天朋友们为他举行了送别晚会。大家都喝了很多酒。回家的时候，因为下雨路滑，马克不小心出了交通事故。车被撞坏了，马克的手也被撞破了。第二天，马克和保险公司联系，可保险公司说车的保险期刚过，不能得到赔款。这真是祸不单行啊！

pinyin: kè, lí, jǔ, hē, hou, huá, kè, jiāo shì gù, bèi zhuàng, kè, bèi, zhuàng, dì, kè, bǎoxiǎn, lián xì, bǎoxiǎn, bǎoxiǎn, gāng, zhēn, huò, a

5. Writing（写汉字）:

十 土 土 扌 圹 圹 垍 垍 堵 堵 堵 堵　　(318)
堵 堵 堵 堵 堵

十 土 圹 均 均 均 均　　(319)
均 均 均 均 均

十 土 圹 圹 圹 址 址　　(320)
址 址 址 址 址

130

# Unit 28

一 干 开 开 刑 刑 型 型 型 (321)

型 型 型 型 型

十 土 土 圤 圹 垃 垃 培 培 培 (322)

培 培 培 培 培

十 土 土 圤 圹 圹 坮 坮 增 增 增 增 (323)

增 增 增 增 增

又 又 圣 圣 圣 (324)

圣 圣 圣 圣 圣

十 土 土 圤 坏 坏 坏 (325)

坏 坏 坏 坏 坏

冂 冂 贝 贝 (326)

贝 贝 贝 贝 贝

一 二 弓 弓 弗 弗 费 费 费 (327)

费 费 费 费 费

厂厂厂斤斤斤所质质质 (328)

质 质 质 质 质

丶丷丷次次次次咨资资 (329)

资 资 资 资 资

丨丨丬丬半半半半半赏赏赏 (330)

赏 赏 赏 赏 赏

冂冂贝贝贝丨贝丨贴贴贴 (331)

贴 贴 贴 贴 贴

一十牛牛失失失失赞赞赞赞赞赞 (332)

赞 赞 赞 赞 赞

冂冂贝贝贝丶贝丶贝亠赔赔赔赔 (333)

赔 赔 赔 赔 赔

一丆石石石 (334)

石 石 石 石 石

# Unit 28

一 厂 丆 石 石 码 码 码 (335)

码 码 码 码 码

一 厂 丆 石 石 矿 矿 矿 砕 砕 碎 碎 碎 (336)

碎 碎 碎 碎 碎

一 厂 丆 石 石 矿 矿 破 破 破 (337)

破 破 破 破 破

丶 冫 氵 沪 沪 沪 沪 (338)

沪 沪 沪 沪 沪

丷 丷 쓰 쓰 㠯 单 单 单 (339)

单 单 单 单 单

马 马 马 (340)

马 马 马 马 马

乚 乂 女 妈 妈 妈 (341)

妈 妈 妈 妈 妈

133

6. Making flash cards（做汉字卡片）。

# Unit 29

## I  Old radicals and new characters
### 旧部首和新汉字

| shí<br>食(饣)<br>shí zì páng<br>食字旁<br>food |
|---|

- 饮: 饣 + 欠(qiàn) ▶ to drink
  * a man opens his mouth to catch his breath (欠) when he is drinking
  冷饮　饮料(liào)

- 饺: 饣 + 交(jiāo)(sound part) ▶ dumpling
  饺子　水饺

| rì<br>日<br>rì zì páng<br>日字旁<br>sun |
|---|

- 春(chūn): spring
  春天　春节

- 暖(nuǎn): warm
  温暖　暖和(huo)

- 易: 日 + 勿(wù) ▶ to change
  * a lizard changes his color easily, this character is a pictograph of a lizard
  容易　易手

- 旺(wàng): 日 + 王(wáng)(sound part) ▶ flourishing
  旺季　旺销

- 暑(shǔ): 日 + 者(zhě) ▶ hot
  暑热　暑期

- 景(jǐng): 日 + 京(jīng)(sound part) ▶ scenery
  风景　景色

- 旬 (xún) : ten days
  
  上旬　下旬

## Exercises 1（练习一）

1. Choose the correct characters（选择正确的汉字）:

   （1）to drink　　A. 饭　　B. 饮
   （2）spring　　　A. 春　　B. 夏
   （3）warm　　　A. 暖　　B. 暧
   （4）scenery　　A. 景　　B. 晾
   （5）ten days　　A. 句　　B. 旬

2. Reading（读一读,认汉字）:

饮料(liào)　什么饮料(liào)　喝(hē)什么饮料(liào)　想喝(hē)什么饮料(liào)　你想喝(hē)什么饮料(liào)？

饺子　包饺子　不会包饺子　我不会包饺子,只会吃饺子。

春天　春天来了　冬天走了,春天来了。

暖和(huo)　天气暖和(huo)了　春天来了,天气暖和(huo)了。

交(jiāo)易(jiāo)　交易所　房屋(wū)交易所　在房屋(wū)交易所
他们在房屋(wū jiāo)交易所办手续。

暑假　每年暑假　上大学后每年暑假我都去超市打工。

景色　这里的景色　把这里的景色照(zhào)下来
我要把这里的景色都照(zhào)下来。

旺季　旅游(yóu)的旺季　五月和十月是旅游(yóu)的旺季。

上旬或(zhě)者下旬　一月下旬或(zhě)者二月上旬
春节在一月下旬或(zhě)者二月上旬。

# II  New radicals and characters
## 新部首和新汉字

| fù |
|---|
| 阜 |
| zuǒ ěr duǒ |
| (阝—左耳朵) |
| hill |

- 院<sup>yuàn</sup>：阝＋完<sup>wán</sup>(sound part) ▶institute
  学院　院子
- 除<sup>chú</sup>：阝＋余<sup>yú</sup>(sound part) ▶except
  除了　除名
- 附<sup>fù</sup>：阝＋付<sup>fù</sup>(sound part) ▶attached
  附上　附近
- 险<sup>xiǎn</sup>：阝＋佥<sup>qiān</sup>(sound part) ▶risk
  风险　危险<sup>wēi</sup>
- 阴<sup>yīn</sup>：阝＋月<sup>yuè</sup> ▶overcast
  阴天　阴阳

| shān |
|---|
| 山 |
| shān zì páng |
| 山字旁 |
| mountain |

- 岛<sup>dǎo</sup>：鸟<sup>niǎo</sup>(sound part)＋山 ▶island
  * sea-birds often nest on an island, which is a mountainous rocks in the sea
  冰岛　岛国
- 岁<sup>suì</sup>：山＋夕<sup>xī</sup> ▶age
  岁月　几岁

| xī |
|---|
| 夕 |
| xī zì páng |
| 夕字旁 |
| evening |

- 外<sup>wài</sup>：夕＋卜<sup>bǔ</sup> ▶out
  国外　外面
- 夜<sup>yè</sup>：亠＋亻＋夕＋ヽ ▶night
  * a person is sleeping under cover in the evening
  夜晚　半夜

## Exercises 2（练习二）

1. Choose the correct characters（选择正确的汉字）：

   （1）except　　A. 际　　B. 除
   （2）attached　　A. 阿　　B. 附
   （3）overcast　　A. 阴　　B. 阳
   （4）island　　A. 鸟　　B. 岛
   （5）out　　A. 外　　B. 处

2. Reading（读一读，认汉字）：

   院子　把院子打扫干净　我把院子打扫干净了。
   （sǎo）　　　　　　　　　　（sǎo）

   除了　除了星期天　除了星期天我每天去健身房锻炼一个小时。

   附件　附件打不开　邮件收到了，但是附件打不开。
   （jiàn）（jiàn）　　（yóu jiàn shōu）　　（jiàn）

   保险　哪种保险　哪种保险好　哪种保险好？给我推荐一个。
   （bǎo）　（bǎo）　　（bǎo）　　　（bǎo）　　　　　　（jiàn）

   阴　阴有时有雨　多云转阴有时有雨　今天下午多云转阴有时有雨。

   岛　海南岛　海南岛的风景　海南岛的风景很美。
   　　　　　　　　　　　　　　　　　　　（měi）

   几岁　几岁上学　应该几岁上学　中国人应该几岁上学？
   　　　　　　　　（gāi）　　　　（gāi）

   精力　没有精力　没有精力学习汉语　工作太忙了，没有精力学习汉语。
   　　　　　　　　　　　　　　　　　　　（máng）

   外面　搬到外面去　把桌子搬到外面去　请你把桌子搬到外面去。
   （bān）　　（zhuō bān）　　　（zhuō bān）

   夜　三夜　三天三夜　三天三夜讲不完　他们的故事三天三夜也讲不完。
   　　　　　　　　　　　　　　　　（gù shì）

## III  Sound parts
## 声旁

青 green (qīng) + 忄 = 情 emotion (qíng)    感情

+ 氵 = 清 clear (qīng)    清水

+ 日 = 晴 sunny (qíng)    晴天

+ 目 = 睛 eye (jīng)    眼睛

+ 虫 = 蜻 dragonfly (qīng)    蜻蜓 (tíng)

+ 争 = 静 quiet (jìng)    安静

+ 米 = 精 refined (jīng)    精力

### Exercises 3（练习三）

1. Combine the radicals and the sound part into characters, then match their English meaning（用所给部首和声旁组成汉字并与英文匹配）：

   日　　　　　　dragonfly
   虫　　　　　　sunny
   忄　　　　　　refined
   氵　　青　　　emotion
   米　　　　　　clear
   目　　　　　　eye
   争　　　　　　quiet

2. Please write down other characters with this sound part（用上面的声旁再组几个汉字）：

_____

Unit 29

139

# IV Homework
## 课后作业

1. Choose the correct radicals（选择正确的偏旁）:
   - （1）yǐn (to drink)　　　A. 口　B. 饣
   - （2）shǔ (hot)　　　　　A. 日　B. 皿
   - （3）wàng (flourishing)　A. 日　B. 目
   - （4）xiǎn (to risk)　　　A. 阝　B. 月
   - （5）suì (age)　　　　　A. 山　B. 出
   - （6）yè (night)　　　　　A. 夕　B. 夂

2. Find the correct pinyin and meaning for the given characters（找找所给汉字正确的拼音和意思）:

   院　　　夜　　　饺　　　岛　　　春

   yè　　　yuàn　　　dǎo　　　jiǎo　　　chūn

3. Circle the phrases with the characters you have learned as many as you can（用所给汉字组成尽可能多的短语）:

   | 春 | 冷 | 饮 | 旺 | 季 | 易 |
   |---|---|---|---|---|---|
   | 暖 | 风 | 景 | 附 | 上 | 旬 |
   | 阴 | 险 | 院 | 岁 | 小 | 岛 |
   | 除 | 外 | 饺 | 子 | 夜 | 暑 |

   1. 春风　　2. _____　　3. _____
   4. _____　5. _____　　6. _____
   7. _____　8. _____　　9. _____
   10. _____　11. _____　12. _____
   13. _____　14. _____　15. _____

4. Read the following paragraph（读一读，认汉字）:

   　　中国有很多传tǒng统的节日。在这xiē些节日里，春节是最zuì大最zuì热闹的。春节在每年的阴历正月初一，它tā是阴历旧jiù年的结束shù、新xīn年的开始。

   　　新xīn年前，家家都要把房子打扫sǎo干净。新xīn年的前一天晚wǎn上叫"大年夜"，也叫"除夕"。全家人应该在一起吃年夜饭,然后看电视、放鞭炮、听钟声,高兴地等待新年的到来。平时,大家工作都很忙,没有时间走亲访友,春节放假的时间特别长,亲朋好友正好可以在一起聚聚。不过,去拜年的时候,最好带一点礼物,特别是别忘了给孩子们压岁钱。

每年春节,大家要花很多时间和精力去买东西、做好吃的、打扫房间、走亲访友、招待亲友,休息的时间反而比较少。所以,过年以后,人们见面常常说"很累",可是第二年春节还是这么过。

在你们的国家,最大最热闹的节日是什么?还有什么别的节日?有什么习俗?你最喜欢的节日是什么?

## 5. Writing (写汉字):

饮 (345)

饺 (346)

春 (347)

暖 (348)

冂 冂 曰 曰 昜 易 易 易 (349)
易 易 易 易 易

冂 冂 曰 曰 旦 早 昇 昇 暑 暑 暑 暑 (350)
暑 暑 暑 暑 暑

冂 冂 曰 曰 旦 早 昌 昌 景 景 景 景 (351)
景 景 景 景 景

冂 冂 日 日 日´ 旺 旺 旺 (352)
旺 旺 旺 旺 旺

勹 勹 旬 旬 旬 旬 (353)
旬 旬 旬 旬 旬

丿 广 户 卢 自 自 阜 阜 (354)
阜 阜 阜 阜 阜

阝 阝 阝` 阝宀 阝宀 阝宁 阝完 院 院 (355)
院 院 院 院 院

# Unit 29

| ㄅ ㄅ ㄨ 队 阶 除 除 除 除 | | | | | | | | | | | |
|---|---|---|---|---|---|---|---|---|---|---|---|
(356)

| 除 | 除 | 除 | 除 | 除 | | | | | | | |

| ㄅ ㄅ ㄨ 队 一 附 附 附 | | | | | | | | | | | |
(357)

| 附 | 附 | 附 | 附 | 附 | | | | | | | |

| ㄅ ㄅ ㄨ 队 阶 阶 险 险 险 | | | | | | | | | | | |
(358)

| 险 | 险 | 险 | 险 | 险 | | | | | | | |

| ㄅ ㄅ 阴 阴 阴 阴 | | | | | | | | | | | |
(359)

| 阴 | 阴 | 阴 | 阴 | 阴 | | | | | | | |

| 丨 山 山 | | | | | | | | | | | |
(360)

| 山 | 山 | 山 | 山 | 山 | | | | | | | |

| 勹 勺 鸟 岛 岛 岛 岛 | | | | | | | | | | | |
(361)

| 岛 | 岛 | 岛 | 岛 | 岛 | | | | | | | |

| 丨 山 屮 岁 岁 岁 | | | | | | | | | | | |
(362)

| 岁 | 岁 | 岁 | 岁 | 岁 | | | | | | | |

ク夕夕
夕 夕 夕 夕 夕

ク夕夕外外
外 外 外 外 外

亠广广疒疒夜夜
夜 夜 夜 夜 夜

一 = 三 丰 青 青 青 青
青 青 青 青 青

丶 忄 忄 忄 忄 忄 情 情 情 情
情 情 情 情 情

丶 冫 氵 氵 沣 清 清 清 清 清
清 清 清 清 清

丨 冂 冂 日 日⁻ 日= 旪 晴 晴 晴 晴
晴 晴 晴 晴 晴

| 丨 | 冂 | 月 | 目 | 目 | 日⁻ | 日⁺ | 旷 | 晴 | 晴 | 晴 | 晴 |
|---|---|---|---|---|---|---|---|---|---|---|---|

(370)

| 晴 | 晴 | 晴 | 晴 | 晴 | | | | | | | |
|---|---|---|---|---|---|---|---|---|---|---|---|

| 丨 | 口 | 中 | 虫 | 虫 | 虫⁻ | 虫⁺ | 虫⁺ | 蜻 | 蜻 | 蜻 | 蜻 |
|---|---|---|---|---|---|---|---|---|---|---|---|

(371)

| 蜻 | 蜻 | 蜻 | 蜻 | 蜻 | | | | | | | |
|---|---|---|---|---|---|---|---|---|---|---|---|

| 一 | 十 | 丰 | 丰 | 青 | 青 | 青 | 青⁻ | 青⁺ | 静 | 静 | 静 |
|---|---|---|---|---|---|---|---|---|---|---|---|

(372)

| 静 | 静 | 静 | 静 | 静 | | | | | | | |
|---|---|---|---|---|---|---|---|---|---|---|---|

| 丶 | 丷 | 丬 | 斗 | 米 | 米 | 米 | 米⁺ | 精 | 精 | 精 | 精 |
|---|---|---|---|---|---|---|---|---|---|---|---|

(373)

| 精 | 精 | 精 | 精 | 精 | | | | | | | |
|---|---|---|---|---|---|---|---|---|---|---|---|

6. Making flash cards（做汉字卡片）。

# Unit 30

## I Old radicals and new characters
### 旧部首和新汉字

| mù |
| :---: |
| 木 |
| mù zì páng |
| 木字旁 |
| wood |

- 松 sōng: 木 + 公 gōng (sound part) ▶ pine; loose
  松树　松开 shù

- 某 mǒu: 甘 gān + 木 ▶ certain
  某人　某地

- 条 tiáo: 夂 + 木 zhǐ ▶ strip; measure word
  面条　一条路

- 格 gé: 木 + 各 gè (sound part) ▶ case
  格子　方格

- 柬 jiǎn: note
  请柬　书柬

- 束 shù: to bind; measure word
  约束　结束

- 术 shù: 木 + 、 ▶ skill
  学术　手术

- 查 chá: 木 + 旦 dàn ▶ to check
  查看　查明

- 标 biāo: 木 + 示 shì ▶ mark
  标记　路标

● 本: 木+一 ▶root; measure word
  \* it is a pictograph of a tree with the root
  本来　一本书

● 根: 木+艮(sound part) ▶root
  根本　草根

## Exercises 1（练习一）

**1. Choose the correct characters（选择正确的汉字）:**

(1) certain　　A. 某　　B. 粟
(2) bind　　　A. 柬　　B. 束
(3) skill　　　A. 木　　B. 术
(4) check　　A. 杳　　B. 查
(5) root　　　A. 本　　B. 末

**2. Reading（读一读，认汉字）:**

放松　放松放松　你在电脑前面坐了这么长(cháng)时间了，放松放松吧。

某公司　本市某公司　昨天本市某公司

　　　　昨天本市某公司发生了一起重大事故(shì gù)。

条　一条　一条路　两条鱼　三条蛇(shé)　四条裤(kù)子　五条裙(qún)子　六条围巾

风格　什么风格　喜欢什么风格　你喜欢什么风格的衣服？

请柬(jiǎn)　收到请柬　收到你寄给我的请柬了

　　　你收到我寄给你的请柬(jiǎn)了吗？

一束　一束花　连一束花也没有送过

　　　从认识到结婚他连一束花也没有送过。

技(jì)术　开车技(jì)术　开车技(jì)术不高　我的开车技(jì)术不高，不敢(gǎn)在这里开。

检(jiǎn)查　检(jiǎn)查身体　每年去医院(yī)检(jiǎn)查身体

　　　老(lǎo)年人应该每年去医院(yī)检(jiǎn)查身体。

标(zhǔn)准　说得标(zhǔn)准　把汉语说得标(zhǔn)准　想要把汉语说得标(zhǔn)准不容易。

根本　根本没有　根本没有跟我说过　他根本没有跟我说过。

# II New radicals and characters
## 新部首和新汉字

| 丶 diǎn 点 |
|---|

- 为 / 为 (wéi/wèi) : as; for, to
  作为(wéi)　为(wèi)了

- 举 (jǔ) : to raise
  举起　举手

| 匚 qū zìkuāng 区字框 |
|---|

- 医 : 匚+矢(yī)(shǐ) ▶doctor
  \* man needs a doctor when an arrow is in his body
  医生　医院

- 区 : 匚+乂(qū) ▶section
  市区　时区

| 冂 tóng zìkuāng 同字框 |
|---|

- 内 : 冂+人(nèi)(rén) ▶in
  国内　内部

- 再 (zài) : again
  再见　再三

| 亠 jīng zì tóu 京字头 |
|---|

- 京 : 亠+口+小(jīng) ▶Beijing
  北京　京城

- 享 : 亠+口+子(xiǎng) ▶enjoy
  分享　享用

- 音：立+日  ▶sound
  音乐　口音

  (yīn lì rì)

## Exercises 2 (练习二)

1. Choose the correct characters (选择正确的汉字)：
   (1) for, to　　A. 办　B. 为
   (2) section　　A. 区　B. 冈
   (3) in　　　　A. 内　B. 闪
   (4) again　　 A. 冉　B. 再
   (5) to enjoy  A. 亨　B. 享

2. Reading (读一读，认汉字)：

   因为　　因为……所以……　　因为要工作

   　　因为要工作，所以下学期不能继续学习了。

   举行　　在北京举行　　奥运会在北京举行　　2008年的奥运会在北京举行。

   中医　　看过中医　　我从来没看过中医　　我从来没看过中医，也没吃过中药。

   郊区　　在郊区　　不在市区，在郊区　　我的家不在市区，在郊区。

   市内　　市内电话　　打市内电话　　免费打市内电话

   　　这里可以免费打市内电话。

   再　　再干　　明天再干　　明天再干吧　　今天干不完，明天再干吧。

   分享　　分享一下　　和大家分享一下　　和大家分享一下你的经验吧。

   音乐家　　成为音乐家　　长大成为音乐家。

   　　女儿的理想是长大成为音乐家。

## III  Sound parts
### 声旁

交 (jiāo) cross + 阝 = 郊 (jiāo) suburb     郊区

+ 纟 = 绞 (jiǎo) to twist     绞肉

+ 木 = 校 (xiào) school     学校

校 (jiào) to check, proof reading     校对

+ 月 = 胶 (jiāo) glue     胶水

+ 足 = 跤 (jiāo) tumble     摔跤 (shuāi)

### Exercises 3 (练习三)

1. Combine the radicals and the sound part into characters, then match their English meaning (用所给部首和声旁组成汉字并与英文匹配):

   月　　　　　　glue
   阝　　　　　　to twist
   纟　　交　　　suburb
   木　　　　　　school/ to check
   足　　　　　　tumble

2. Please write down other characters with this sound part (用上面的声旁再组几个汉字):

   _____

## IV  Homework
### 课后作业

1. Choose the correct radicals (选择正确的偏旁):

   (1) sōng (pine)     A. 讠     B. 木
   (2) tiáo (strip)    A. 木     B. 朩

(3) gé (case)      A. 扌    B. 木
(4) gēn (root)     A. 木    B. 足
(5) yī (doctor)    A. 冂    B. 匚
(6) jīng (Beijing) A. 亠    B. 十

2. Find the correct pinyin and meaning for the given characters（找找所给汉字正确的拼音和意思）:

举　　　　　音　　　　　根　　　　　医　　　　　松

gēn　　　　jǔ　　　　sōng　　　　yī　　　　yīn

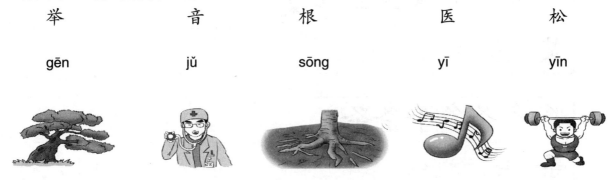

3. Circle the phrases with the characters you have learned as many as you can（用所给汉字组成尽可能多的短语）:

轻 音 根 请 柬 约
松 条 标 本 为 来
举 格 某 区 再 京
医 院 校 内 查 术

1. 轻松　　　2. _____　　　3. _____
4. _____　　4. _____　　　6. _____
7. _____　　8. _____　　　9. _____
10. _____　 11. _____　　 12. _____
13. _____　 14. _____　　 15. _____

4. Read the following paragraph（读一读，认汉字）:

　　马克下个星期就要回国了。今天李大明给马克上了最后一次的汉语辅导课。马克非常感谢李大明对他的帮助，还说了很多他学习汉语的感想。李大明希望马克回国后能继续学习汉语。他还告诉马克学习汉语没有秘诀，只有靠多听、多说、多写、多练。

　　你也学习了一年的汉语了，有什么感想呢？你觉得汉语里哪一个部分最难呢？你学习汉语的时候有什么秘诀吗？说出来，和大家一起分享一下吧。

Chinese with Me: A Chinese Character Course Book(II)

5. Writing (写汉字):

十 十 才 木 朩 杉 松 松 (374)
松 松 松 松 松

一 十 廿 甘 甘 苷 苷 某 某 (375)
某 某 某 某 某

ノ 夂 冬 冬 乆 条 条 (376)
条 条 条 条 条

十 十 才 木 朩 杦 柊 柊 格 格 (377)
格 格 格 格 格

一 一 一 币 币 秉 秉 秉 秉 (378)
秉 秉 秉 秉 秉

一 一 一 币 币 束 束 (379)
束 束 束 束 束

十 十 木 木 术 术 (380)
术 术 术 术 术

| 十 | 十 | 木 | 木 | 杏 | 杏 | 杳 | 査 | 查 | | (381) |

| 查 | 查 | 查 | 查 | 查 | | | | | | |

| 十 | 才 | 才 | 木 | 村 | 标 | 标 | 标 | 标 | | (382) |

| 标 | 标 | 标 | 标 | 标 | | | | | | |

| 十 | 才 | 木 | 本 | 本 | | | | | | (383) |

| 本 | 本 | 本 | 本 | 本 | | | | | | |

| 十 | 才 | 才 | 木 | 札 | 杞 | 杞 | 根 | 根 | 根 | (384) |

| 根 | 根 | 根 | 根 | 根 | | | | | | |

| ノ | 力 | 为 | 为 | | | | | | | (385) |

| 为 | 为 | 为 | 为 | 为 | | | | | | |

| 丶 | 丷 | 兴 | 兴 | 兴 | 兴 | 举 | 举 | | | (386) |

| 举 | 举 | 举 | 举 | 举 | | | | | | |

| 一 | 厂 | 匚 | 乒 | 乓 | 医 | 医 | | | | (387) |

| 医 | 医 | 医 | 医 | 医 | | | | | | |

| 一 | 又 | 区 | 区 | | | | | | | (388) |

| 区 | 区 | 区 | 区 | 区 | | | | | | |

冂 内 内 内
内 内 内 内 内
(389)

厂 厂 丙 丙 再 再
再 再 再 再 再
(390)

亠 亠 六 古 亨 亨 京 京
京 京 京 京 京
(391)

亠 亠 六 古 亨 亨 享 享
享 享 享 享 享
(392)

亠 亠 六 立 立 产 音 音 音
音 音 音 音 音
(393)

亠 亠 六 宀 交 交
交 交 交 交 交
(394)

亠 亠 六 宀 交 交 郊 郊
郊 郊 郊 郊 郊
(395)

纟 纟 纟 纟 纟 纹 纹 绞 绞 (396)

绞 绞 绞 绞 绞

十 才 才 木 术 杧 杧 杧 校 校 (397)

校 校 校 校 校

丿 月 月 月 刖 肑 肑 肑 胶 胶 (398)

胶 胶 胶 胶 胶

丨 口 口 口 足 足 足 趵 趵 趵 跤 跤 (399)

跤 跤 跤 跤 跤

6. Making flash cards（做汉字卡片）。

# Appendix 1

# Keys to Exercises
# 练习参考答案

## Unit 16

**Exercises 1**
B A B B B

**Exercises 2**
B A A B B

**Homework**
1. A B A B B B
3. 很对 很大 很小 大小 大姐 小姐 不会 不行 不要 银行 几位 导游 开会 开始

## Unit 17

**Exercises 1**
A B B B A

**Exercises 2**
A B A B A B

**Homework**
1. A B B A B B
3. 天气 下雨 下雪 港口 空气 气温 雨水 酒水 潮湿 平时 干净 温水 集中 零钱

## Unit 18

**Exercises 1**
B A A B B

**Exercises 2**
A A B C B

**Homework**
1. B A B B B A
3. 哪儿 所有 所以 房子 生病 几号 几路 病人 首先 身体 其中 失去 至于 人体

## Unit 19

**Exercises 1**
A B A B A

**Exercises 2**
A A A B B

**Homework**
1. A B B B B A
3. 每天 送行 运动 运动会 正步 航海 海边 行动 退步 刀疤 一边 加法 度过 办公

# Appendix 1  Keys to Exercises

## Unit 20

**Exercises 1**
B A A B C

**Exercises 2**
A B A A C

**Homework**
1. A B A B A
3. 轻轨  发电  超越  改正  导电  证人  前面  正面  正反  放心  亲自  效果  反面  由于

## Unit 21

**Exercises 1**
A B A A B

**Exercises 2**
B A A A B

**Homework**
1. B A B A B A
3. 意见  白色  感动  总是  双色  双眼  后悔  看上  失业  失重  失眠  重量  上网  无业

## Unit 22

**Exercises 1**
B B A A B

**Exercises 2**
B A A A B

**Homework**
1. A B B B B
3. 成人  成才  讨论  全面  全职  面试  人才  战争  竞争  答应  应聘  简便  回答  讲话

## Unit 23

**Exercises 1**
A A A B B

**Exercises 2**
A B A C C B

**Homework**
1. B B A A B
3. 报复  复习  预习  额头  申请  支出  出口  入口  头号  挑战  挂号  担心  招收  顺心

## Unit 24

**Exercises 1**
A B A A B

**Exercises 2**
B A B B A

**Homework**
1. B B A B B A
3. 私人  人民  民族  秋季  欢欣  不多  不常  四季  稍后  旅行  多次  常常  歌后  行程

## Unit 25

**Exercises 1**
B B A B A

**Exercises 2**
B A A A B

**Homework**
1. A A A B B A
3. 电线  幸福  续约  喜欢  祝福  约会  细纱  首都  都会  部门  热闹  热门  书社  礼炮

## Unit 26

**Exercises 1**
A A A B B

**Exercises 2**
A A A A B

**Homework**
1. B A B A B B
3. 包围 获得 药用 团结 结实 安定 用完 请客 实力 节约 约定 完成 风力 花茶

## Unit 27

**Exercises 1**
A A B B A

**Exercises 2**
A B B B A

**Homework**
1. B A A B A B
3. 剧本 原本 原理 来历 来到 肯定 副本 本来 本能 别人 电脑 专利 利息 服气

## Unit 28

**Exercises 1**
B B B A A

**Exercises 2**
A B B A B

**Homework**
1. B A A B B A
3. 堵车 欣赏 坏车 车费 车型 车号 均码 破碎 型号 号码 赔款 单号 投资 资金

## Unit 29

**Exercises 1**
B A A A B

**Exercises 2**
B B A B A

**Homework**
1. B A A A A
3. 冷饮 冷风 旺季 暖风 风景 风险 附上 上旬 阴险 院子 小岛 除外 饺子 子夜

## Unit 30

**Exercises 1**
A B B B A

**Exercises 2**
B A A B B

**Homework**
1. B B B A B A
3. 音标 根本 请柬 约束 松条 标本 某区 某院 某校 区内 医院 院校 校内 校区

# Appendix 2

# Translations for Reference
# 参考译文

**Notes:**

* This part is the translations for last sentences in each unit's reading exercises. (下面是各单元"读一读，认汉字"部分最后一句的英译)

## Unit 16

I.
1. Does the company hold the congress in the afternoon?
2. How many guests are there in the restaurant?
3. Do you believe him or not?
4. On Sunday entire family has the lunch at home.
5. I want to study Chinese culture.
6. She has an elder sister, I do not have one.
7. If it does not rain, I will come.
8. When will you start to study Chinese?
9. Should I call him or not?

II.
1. Did I say correctly? You said very correctly.
2. We want a tour guide who can speak English.
3. He speaks Chinese very well.
4. My bicycle is very new, his bicycle is not.
5. Do you know where the bank is? The bank is not on the left, it is on the right.
6. My wife and I want to study China's law.
7. China has a very long history.

## Unit 17

I.
1. My home is clean, his home is not clean.
2. From December to February are Shanghai's winter, Shanghai's winter is cold.
3. I take bus to the company every day.
4. Hong Kong's harbor is very busy every day.
5. I can't drink too much alcohol.
6. French's grammar is difficult very much.

7. Shanghai's summer is humid, Beijing's summer is not.

8. Today's highest temperature is 30 degrees, and the lowest temperature is 22 degrees.

9. Shanghai is China's coastal city.

II.

1. The air there is always very fresh.

2. There has little rain every day in this week.

3. Weather forecast says it will snow tomorrow.

4. The score of the match tonight is zero to zero.

5. Everybody, please gather together, I have some words to say.

6. She not only can speak Chinese but also speaks very well.

7. My daughter is usually very busy in study, and has little time to play.

## Unit 18

I.

1. Where are you from? Where do you live? Where do you work?

2. What's the date of today? What day is today? Today is April 10th, Wednesdays.

3. Please do not spit everywhere.

4. Smoking isn't allowed in some public places.

5. Beijing is dryer than Shanghai.

6. I did exercises every day before I came to Shanghai, I don't do exercises every day after I came to Shanghai.

II.

1. Do you have Shanghai registered permanent residence? I don't have Shanghai registered permanent residence.

2. Because I don't have Shanghai registered permanent residence, I have to do the procedure.

3. How many rooms in this house are facing to the south?

4. I am not ill, just a little uncomfortable.

5. Turn left at the next intersection.

6. She goes shopping with me together.

7. He runs much faster than me.

8. I am Japanese, other classmates are the westerners.

9. If you get up early and sleep early every day, you will be very health.

10. You are my friend, I can't lose that.

11. First......Secondly......Finally......

12. I want to travel next month, as for the place I haven't decided yet.

## Unit 19

I.

1. Everybody should go home to celebrate the New Year during Spring Festival.

2. I often watch the television while eating dinner.

3. May I drive you home?

4. This question is too difficult, even teacher did not know.

5. To return a ticket is easy, but to buy a ticket is difficult.

6. Human's normal body temperature is 37 degrees.

7. You should certainly do what you promised others.

# Appendix 2   Translations for Reference

**II.**
1. I want to thank to those who helped me.
2. My favorite sport is running.
3. Is Mr. Wang still in the office to work overtime?
4. We are having Chinese lesson now.
5. My parents both work in the Airline.
6. Every student, please introduce yourself.
7. I grew up at the sea side.

## Unit 20

**I.**
1. I want to look for a Chinese tutor.
2. I take the light rail to go to the school every morning.
3. There is a big supermarket nearby my home.
4. You write Chinese characters better and better.
5. Do not be too tired at work.
6. Because of everybody's effort, the work is completed ahead of time.
7. Make a phone call / answer the phone / hang up the phone / the line is busy

**II.**
1. My thought is opposite to yours.
2. Have you received the email I sent to you?
3. Where do I put these things? Put these things there.
4. Xiao Wang's work is highly effective.
5. That company changed the name recently.
6. Ahead is my home, do not see me off.
7. He told me this personally.
8. You should do your own thing by yourself.

## Unit 21

**I.**
1. What does this sentence mean?
2. Today will rain, do not forget to take the umbrella.
3. The story you said is very touching.
4. Why is he sometimes hot and sometimes cold to me?
5. He is always very busy, even on Sunday he doesn't rest.
6. The wallet is lost, I'm really worried.
7. It is pointless to regret it now.
8. Have a good rest if you got sick.
9. There are many ways to do body exercises.
10. How are this month's sales?

**II.**
1. Many people like white color.
2. What do you think how to solve this problem?
3. Why do I suffer from insomnia recently?
4. Her eyes are very big, but her eyesight is bad.

5. This box weights 20 kilograms.

6. May I have free internet here?

7. After work, he could not sleep late.

8. Wherever I go, I won't forget you, my friends.

9. Today's homework is very difficult, I have not done yet.

## Unit 22

I.

1. May I ask why do you apply for this position?

2. Thanks a lot for your help.

3. Please tell your classmates there's no school tomorrow.

4. This question needs to be discussed again.

5. If you pass the trial class test, you can become our center's teacher.

6. Our company trains new staffs every year.

7. That company recruits a sales manager, I want to go to try.

II.

1. You may come either on Monday or Tuesday.

2. It will be nice if there was no war.

3. At the same time of the competition, they have become good friends.

4. You should get off at the next stop.

5. Please answer this question.

6. This question is really too simple.

7. Even such a simple question you have calculated wrong.

8. He is a rare talented person.

9. Which aspect do you think is most important?

10. He will become a father soon.

## Unit 23

I.

1. Everybody did well in yesterday's test.

2. Every morning I read the newspaper while drinking a coffee.

3. The buses are very crowded during the rush hours.

4. There writes a character "Tui" (push) on the gate of the bank.

5. The people who come to Shanghai to invest are getting more and more.

6. I want to look for a challenging job.

7. I do not know that person who beckons me.

8. There is a picture hanging on the wall.

9. Your application has already been approved.

II.

1. June to August is Shanghai's summer, Shanghai's summer is very hot.

2. The advantage of riding a bicycle is the time relatively free.

3. You should preview before the class, and review after the class.

4. This card's overdraw amount is 2000 US dollars.

5. Wish you everything goes smoothly.

6. How much is the income and outcome per month?

# Appendix 2  Translations for Reference

7. I want to go to the bank to apply for a credit card.

8. This medicine should be taken before meal.

## Unit 24

I.

1. Yesterday morning I took a taxi to go to the company.
2. Autumn has come, the weather is getting cold.
3. The number you dialed is power off, please dial again later.
4. The people who buy private cars are getting more and more.
5. Teacher is a stable occupation.
6. I want to look at tomorrow's traveling schedule.
7. There has four seasons in one year. They are spring, summer, autumn and winter.

II.

1. I like to travel together with my friends, not with tour group.
2. How does she sing? She sings very well.
3. How many times have you been to China? I have been to China for seven times.
4. Many young people ask for the loan from the bank to buy a house.
5. He appreciates music while drinking red wine.
6. China has 56 nationalities.
7. I want to buy a big scarf for the winter.
8. The teacher often asks us questions.

## Unit 25

I.

1. The night here is very lively.
2. I have to work overtime at the company today so I cannot date with my girlfriend.
3. You may absolutely feel relieved for our company's products.
4. Have you finished all the procedures?
5. Please call our hot line if you have any questions.
6. I want to go to Suzhou to buy some silks to give my friends.
7. Please speak it in detail.
8. He has married twice.
9. The bride wears a white wedding dress.

II.

1. China's capital is in Beijing. / Beijing is China's capital.
2. These books are for you.
3. The first half part of the novel writes much better than the second half one.
4. The groom drank much alcohol on the wedding ceremony.
5. I watched one afternoon television yesterday.
6. The university students should go to the society to practice earlier.
7. I sincerely bless you.
8. This is my first time to take part in Chinese wedding.
9. This is my favorite book.
10. Marriage is a big happy event in one's life.
11. She said that she is the happiest person.

## Unit 26

**I.**
1. This time we don't travel with a tour group.
2. Why so many people encircle there?
3. It is very easy to catch a cold in such weather.
4. Goes to work happily, goes home safely.
5. As soon as I finish the class, I will go to your home.
6. Tomorrow he certainly will come. / Tomorrow he certainly will not come. / Tomorrow he will not certainly come.
7. I invited 50 guests to attend the party.
8. The school dormitory's fee is not expensive.
9. I really have no time to travel.

**II.**
1. It is very expensive to buy flowers in the holiday.
2. Try the traditional Chinese medicine if the western medicine is not useful.
3. The Spring Festival is the biggest and most lively holiday in China.
4. Do you know the opening hours of that shop?
5. He got the first place in the running match of the sports game.
6. Drinking tea is very good for the body.
7. I write a letter to him to express my gratitude.
8. On the first day of New Year I should go to parents' home to pay a New Year visit.
9. I like to wear silk shirt in the summer.
10. I still don't know how to use the chopsticks to eat.
11. Study hard and make progress every day.

## Unit 27

**I.**
1. The life in China is a very interesting experience.
2. Originally you are the brother of Xiao Wang.
3. She is so that she can speak five languages.
4. My face turns red as soon as I drink alcohol.
5. I promise my parents this time I definitely will go home to celebrate the New Year.
6. It is not allowed to speak loudly in the library.
7. This clothes is not washed cleanly.
8. My mother asks me to teach her how to use the computer.

**II.**
1. I will call you after I arrive at home.
2. I want to go to other places to have a look.
3. a pair of earrings / a pair of gloves / a pair of eyeglasses
4. Even Chinese people cannot understand the Peking opera.
5. You must make use of this opportunity to study well.
6. There are 28 students in our class.
7. It is very difficult to manage such a big company well.
8. My dream is to do a round-world trip.
9. Present's life is much richer than the past.

# Appendix 2　Translations for Reference

10. Listen to the music can make people happy.

## Unit 28

I.
1. Because of the traffic jam, today I was late again.
2. The average lifetime of Chinese women is 80 years old.
3. Please write down your address here.
4. This is the newest model that the company just promoted.
5. The parents want to bring up the children into talented person.
6. The house rent increased again this month.
7. Christmas is very important to many country's people.
8. My bicycle has gone bad, can you repair it?

II.
1. I guess the expense of study overseas must be very expensive.
2. I think the quality is the most important thing when I go shopping.
3. This project needs amount of fund.
4. At Mid-Autumn Festival's evening entire family enjoys looking at the moon together.
5. There is a China map sticking on the wall of the classroom.
6. The Chinese people say "nali, nali" (means "no, no") when they are praised by others.
7. Why can't I get the indemnity?
8. Could you tell me your telephone number?
9. My mother's favorite vase was broken by me.
10. My finger was cut by the knife.
11. "Hu" is Shanghai's abbreviation. / Shanghai's abbreviation is "Hu".
12. He is still single so far.

## Unit 29

I.
1. What drink do you want to drink?
2. I don't know how to wrap dumplings, I only know how to eat them.
3. Winter has gone, spring is coming.
4. Spring has come, the weather is getting warm.
5. They are doing procedures in Housing Exchange.
6. After going to the college, every summer vacation I go to supermarket to work part time.
7. I will take pictures of the scenery here.
8. May and October are the hot seasons of the traveling.
9. Spring Festival in late January or early February.

II.
1. I cleaned up the yard.
2. I go to the gymnasium to exercise for one hour every day except for Sunday.
3. I have received the email, but I could not open the attachment.
4. Which insurance is better? Please recommend one to me.
5. It is cloudy to overcast with rain sometimes this afternoon.
6. Hainan Island's scenery is very beautiful.
7. How old should Chinese people go to school?

8. The work was too busy, I have no energy to study Chinese.
9. Please move the table to the outside.
10. Their stories cannot be finished for three days and three nights.

## Unit 30

**I.**
1. You have sat at the front of the computer for such a long time in, do relax.
2. A serious accident happened in a certain company in this city yesterday.
3. one road / two fish / three snakes / four trousers / five skirts / six scarves
4. What style of the clothes do you like?
5. Have you received the invitation I sent to you?
6. He has never given me a bunch of flowers from knowing to marrying.
7. My driving skill is not good, I do not dare to drive here.
8. The old people should go to the hospital to check their bodies every year.
9. It is not easy to speak standard Chinese.
10. He didn't tell me at all.

**II.**
1. Because of the work, I can't continue to study next semester.
2. Olympic 2008 was held in Beijing.
3. I have never see a traditional Chinese doctor and taken the traditional Chinese medicine either.
4. My home is not in the urban district, it is in the suburb.
5. You may make free local call here.
6. If you can't finish today, do it tomorrow.
7. Could you share your experience with everybody?
8. Daughter's ideal is to become a musician.

# Appendix 3

# Characters Taught in Each Unit
# 每单元所教汉字

**Notes:**

* 407 characters and radicals in total, of which radicals and their corresponding character forms are shown in bold.
* What in brackets are forms of radicals when they appear in other characters.
* The number following each character stands for the unit in which the character appears in *Chinese with me: An Integrated Course Book*.

**OR & NC** = Old radicals & new characters  **NR & C** = New radicals & characters
**OC** = Other characters   **SP & C** = Sound part & characters

| Unit 16 | OR & NC | 人(亻)1 | 会5/27 | 位6 | 信15/23 | 全16 | 化16 | 件8/23 |
|---|---|---|---|---|---|---|---|---|
| | | 女1 | 姐5 | 如7/18 | 始11 | 要16 | | |
| | NR & C | 寸 | 对2/22 | 导16 | 彳 | 很1 | 行6/7/24 | 得8/27 律16 |
| | OC | 史16 | | | | | | |
| 24 | SP & C | 主10/22 | 住14/24 | 拄 | 注17 | 柱 | | |
| Unit 17 | OR & NC | 冫5 | 净13 | 冬17 | | | | |
| | | 氵5 | 汽3 | 港6 | 酒14/25 | 法16 | 潮17 湿17 | 温17 沿17 |
| | NR & C | 气6/17 | 穴7/17 | 空7/17 | 雨17 | 雪17 | 零17 | 隹 难15 集17 |
| | OC | 而15/17 | 平17 | | | | | |
| 27 | SP & C | 分6/17 | 份 | 吩 | 纷 | 氛 | 粉 | |
| Unit 18 | OR & NC | 口3 | 哪1 | 号7/22 | 吐 | 吸22 | 火(灬)2 | 燥17 炼18 |
| | NR & C | 户23 | 所16 | 房9/18 | 广 | 病18 | 足(⻊) | 路3 跟7 跑18 |
| | OC | 其18 | 身18 | 失18 | 首18 | 至18 | 于18 | |
| 26 | SP & C | 方3/18 | 仿 | 访20 | 妨 | 纺 | | |
| Unit 19 | OR & NC | 辶7 | 过5/22 | 边6 | 送16 | 运18 | 连19 | 退19 通3/22 |
| | | 广6 | 度11/17 | 应13/19/22 | | | | |

167

|  |  |  |  |  |  |  |  |  |  |
|---|---|---|---|---|---|---|---|---|---|
|  | NR & C | 力21 | 助7 | 动18 | 办19 | 加19 | 止 | 正5/17 | 步18 | 舟 | 航19 |
|  | OC | 父19 | 母19 | 每7 | 海17 |  |  |  |  |
| 28 | SP & C | 巴 | 把29 | 吧4/14 | 爸 | 疤 |  |  |  |
| Unit 20 | OR & NC | 车14 | 辅16 | 轻14/20 | 轨20 | 较13 | 走14 | 超4 | 越20 |
|  |  | 田4 | 累16 | 由20 | 电4/21 |  |  |  |  |
|  | NR & C | 又 | 反17 | 发3/20 | 攵 | 放13/16 | 效18 | 改20 | 收22 |
|  | OC | 前14/20 | 亲12/20 | 自20 |  |  |  |  |  |
| 25 | SP & C | (正5/17) | 证23 | 怔 | 征 | 政 | 症 |  |  |
| Unit 21 | OR & NC | 心(忄)6 | 意5/17 | 忘16 | 感17 | 忽17 | 总17 | 急19 | 悔21 | 息21 |
|  |  | 金(钅)6 | 锻18 | 销21 |  |  |  |  |  |
|  | NR & C | 刀(刂) | 色18 | 免21 | 目 | 看8 | 眠18 | 眼21 | 里 | 重16 | 量21 |
|  | OC | 后21 | 网21 | 无21 | 业21 |  |  |  |  |
| 29 | SP & C | 肖 | 削 | 宵 | 消21 | 霄 |  |  |  |
| Unit 22 | OR & NC | 讠12 | 请3/23 | 谢5 | 诉6 | 讨21 | 论21 | 讲22 | 试8/22 | 训22 |
|  |  | 耳15 | 聘22 | 职22 |  |  |  |  |  |
|  | NR & C | 戈 | 或8 | 成22 | 战22 | 立 | 站6 | 竞22 |  |
|  |  | 竹(⺮) | 答19 | 算8/20 | 简22 |  |  |  |  |
|  | OC | 才22 | 当5/22 | 面2/22 | 就22 |  |  |  |  |
| 29 | SP & C | 争22 | 挣 | 睁 | 筝 |  |  |  |  |
| Unit 23 | OR & NC | 手(扌)8 | 挺16 | 报17 | 挤20 | 推14/21 | 投22 | 挑22 | 招22 | 挂23 | 批23 |
|  |  | 拉 |  |  |  |  |  |  |  |
|  | NR & C | 夂 | 夏17 | 处18 | 复23 | 页 | 预10/18 | 额23 | 顺23 |
|  | OC | 入23 | 申23 | 支23 | 之23 |  |  |  |  |
| 27 | SP & C | 旦29 | 但20 | 担11/23 | 胆 | 疸 |  |  |  |
| Unit 24 | OR & NC | 禾4 | 租3 | 秋18 | 稍20 | 私20 | 稳23 | 程24 | 季24 |
|  | NR & C | 欠 | 欢2 | 歌11 | 次3/18 | 款21 | 欣24 | (方)3/18 | 旅13/24 | 族24 |
|  |  | 巾26 | 师1/16 | 常5/17 |  |  |  |  |  |
|  | OC | 民6/24 |  |  |  |  |  |  |  |
| 25 | SP & C | 羊 | 详24 | 洋 | 样7/17 | 氧 | 痒 |  |  |

# Appendix 3   Characters Taught in Each Unit

| Unit 25 | OR & NC | 门 15 | 闹 25 | | | | | | |
| --- | --- | --- | --- | --- | --- | --- | --- | --- | --- |
| | | 纟 10 | 约 7/20 | 绝 21 | 续 23 | 线 23 | 绸 24 | 细 24 | 结 25 | 纱 25 |
| | NR & C | 邑(阝) | 都 4 | 那 2/18 | 部 19 | 郎 25 | | | | |
| | | 示(礻)26 | 视 9 | 社 24 | 福 25 | 礼 25 | 祝 25 | | | |
| | OC | 书 25 | 喜 2/25 | 幸 25 | | | | | | |
| 29 | SP & C | 包 2/24 | 抱 | 饱 | 泡 | 炮 29 | 雹 | | | |
| Unit 26 | OR & NC | 口 9 | 团 24 | 围 26 | | | | | | |
| | | 宀 2 | 容 17 | 安 18 | 完 12/18 | 定 13/19 | 客 6/23 | 宿 24 | 实 26 | |
| | NR & C | 草(艹) | 花 9 | 药 18 | 节 19 | 营 21 | 获 24 | 茶 26 | | |
| | | 衣(衤) | 表 15/16 | 初 19 | 衬 26 | 衫 26 | | | | |
| | OC | 用 26 | 习 26 | | | | | | | |
| 27 | SP & C | 风 24 | 讽 | 枫 | 疯 | | | | | |
| Unit 27 | OR & NC | 厂 13 | 历 16 | 原 11/19 | 厉 27 | 月 11 | 脸 18 | 肯 19 | 能 21 | 服 2/25 | 脑 27 |
| | NR & C | 刂 | 到 7/16 | 别 5/24 | 副 26 | 剧 27 | 利 5/27 | | | |
| | | 玉(王) | 班 19 | 理 27 | 环 | 球 | | | | |
| | OC | 丰 27 | 乐 27 | | | | | | | |
| 25 | SP & C | 专 27 | 传 29 | 转 | 砖 | | | | | |
| Unit 28 | OR & NC | 土 3 | 堵 12 | 均 17 | 址 20 | 型 21 | 培 22 | 增 22 | 圣 26 | 坏 28 |
| | NR & C | 贝 | 费 21 | 质 21 | 资 22 | 赏 24 | 贴 25 | 赞 26 | 赔 28 | |
| | | 石 | 码 21 | 碎 26 | 破 28 | | | | | |
| | OC | 沪 28 | 单 5/28 | | | | | | | |
| 27 | SP & C | 马 1 | 妈 | 玛 1 | 骂 | 蚂 | | | | |
| Unit 29 | OR & NC | 食(饣)2 | 饮 10 | 饺 29 | | | | | | |
| | | 日 7 | 春 17 | 暖 17 | 易 17 | 暑 22 | 景 24 | 旺 24 | 旬 24 | |
| | NR & C | 阜(阝) | 院 18 | 除 21 | 附 9/23 | 险 28 | 阴 29 | 山 | 岛 24 | 岁 29 |
| | | 夕 29 | 外 9 | 夜 19 | | | | | | |
| | OC | | | | | | | | | |
| 29 | SP & C | 青 | 情 22 | 清 | 晴 | 睛 | 蜻 | 静 18 | 精 29 | |

169

| Unit 30 | OR & NC | 木 8 | 松 16 | 某 22 | 条 23 | 格 24 | 束 25 | 束 25 | 术 27 | 查 28 | 标 30 |
|---|---|---|---|---|---|---|---|---|---|---|---|
| | | 本 30 | 根 30 | | | | | | | | |
| | NR & C | 、 | 为 2/19 | 举 25 | 匚 | 医 18 | 区 30 | 冂 | 内 23 | 再 7/30 | |
| | | 亠 | 京 3/27 | 享 30 | | | | | | | |
| | OC | 音 30 | | | | | | | | | |
| 30 | SP & C | 交 3 | 郊 | 绞 | 校 7 | 胶 | 跤 | | | | |

# Appendix 4

# Index of Characters
# 汉字音序索引

**Notes:**

P = page number of this book

U = unit number of this book in which the character is taught

UI = unit number of *Chinese with Me: An Integrated Course Book* in which the character appears

\* = not selected from *Chinese with Me: An Integrated Course Book*

### A

|  | P | U | UI |
|---|---|---|---|
| 安 ān | 111 | 26 | 18 |

### B

|  | P | U | UI |
|---|---|---|---|
| 吧 ba | 42 | 19 | 4/14 |
| 巴 bā | 42 | 19 | * |
| 疤 bā | 42 | 19 | * |
| 把 bǎ | 42 | 19 | 29 |
| 爸 bà | 42 | 19 | * |
| 班 bān | 122 | 27 | 19 |
| 办 bàn | 40 | 19 | 19 |
| 包 bāo | 103 | 25 | 2/24 |
| 雹 báo | 104 | 25 | * |
| 饱 bǎo | 103 | 25 | * |
| 报 bào | 80 | 23 | 17 |
| 抱 bào | 103 | 25 | * |
| 贝 bèi | 131 | 28 | * |
| 本 běn | 153 | 30 | 30 |
| 边 biān | 39 | 19 | 6 |
| 标 biāo | 153 | 30 | 30 |
| 表 biǎo | 113 | 26 | 15/16 |
| 别 bié | 122 | 27 | 5/24 |
| 病 bìng[1] | 30 | 18 | 18 |
| 步 bù | 41 | 19 | 18 |
| 部 bù | 102 | 25 | 19 |

### C

|  | P | U | UI |
|---|---|---|---|
| 才 cái | 73 | 22 | 22 |
| 草 cǎo[2] | 112 | 26 | * |
| 茶 chá | 113 | 26 | 26 |
| 查 chá | 153 | 30 | 28 |
| 常 cháng | 92 | 24 | 5/17 |
| 超 chāo | 49 | 20 | 4 |
| 潮 cháo | 21 | 17 | 17 |
| 衬 chèn | 20/113 | 26 | 26 |
| 成 chéng | 72 | 22 | 22 |
| 程 chéng | 91 | 24 | 24 |
| 重 chóng[3] | 61 | 21 | 16 |
| 绸 chóu | 101 | 25 | 24 |
| 初 chū | 113 | 26 | 19 |

---

[1] Also see radical form (疒) bìngzìtóu

[2] Also see radical form (艹) cǎozìtóu

[3] Also see radical character (重) zhòng

| | P | U | UI |
|---|---|---|---|
| 除 chú | 142 | 29 | 21 |
| 处 chǔ/chù | 82 | 23 | 18 |
| 传 chuán① | 123 | 27 | 29 |
| 春 chūn | 141 | 29 | 17 |
| 次 cì | 91 | 24 | 13/18 |
| 寸 cùn | 10 | 16 | * |

**D**

| | P | U | UI |
|---|---|---|---|
| 答 dá | 72 | 22 | 19 |
| 担 dān | 84 | 23 | 11/23 |
| 单 dān | 133 | 28 | 5/28 |
| 胆 dǎn | 84 | 23 | * |
| 疸 dǎn | 84 | 23 | * |
| 旦 dàn | 83 | 23 | 29 |
| 但 dàn | 83 | 23 | 20 |
| 刀 dāo② | 60 | 21 | * |
| 导 dǎo | 10 | 16 | 16 |
| 岛 dǎo | 143 | 29 | 24 |
| 到 dào | 121 | 27 | 7/16 |
| 当 dāng/dàng | 73 | 22 | 5/22 |
| 得 de/dé | 10 | 16 | 8/27 |
| 电 diàn | 50 | 20 | 4/21 |
| 定 dìng | 111 | 26 | 13/19 |
| 冬 dōng | 19 | 17 | 17 |
| 动 dòng | 40 | 19 | 18 |
| 都 dōu/dū | 101 | 25 | 4 |
| 堵 dǔ | 130 | 28 | 12 |
| 度 dù | 40 | 19 | 11/17 |
| 锻 duàn | 60 | 21 | 18 |
| 对 duì | 10 | 16 | 2/22 |

**E**

| | P | U | UI |
|---|---|---|---|
| 额 é | 82 | 23 | 23 |
| 而 ér | 21 | 17 | 15/17 |

**F**

| | P | U | UI |
|---|---|---|---|
| 发 fā/fà | 50 | 20 | 3/20 |
| 法 fǎ | 19 | 17 | 16 |
| 反 fǎn | 50 | 20 | 17 |
| 方 fāng | 31 | 18 | 3/18 |
| 房 fáng | 30 | 18 | 9/18 |
| 妨 fáng | 31 | 18 | * |
| 仿 fǎng | 31 | 18 | * |
| 访 fǎng | 31 | 18 | 20 |
| 纺 fǎng | 31 | 18 | * |
| 放 fàng | 50 | 20 | 13/16 |
| 费 fèi | 131 | 28 | 21 |
| 分 fēn | 22 | 17 | 6/17 |
| 吩 fēn | 22 | 17 | * |
| 纷 fēn | 22 | 17 | * |
| 氛 fēn | 22 | 17 | * |
| 粉 fěn | 22 | 17 | * |
| 份 fèn | 22 | 17 | * |
| 丰 fēng | 123 | 27 | 27 |
| 风 fēng | 114 | 26 | 24 |
| 枫 fēng | 114 | 26 | * |
| 疯 fēng | 114 | 26 | * |
| 讽 fěng | 114 | 26 | * |
| 福 fú | 102 | 25 | 25 |
| 服 fú | 121 | 27 | 2/25 |
| 辅 fǔ | 49 | 20 | 16 |
| 副 fù | 122 | 27 | 26 |
| 附 fù | 143 | 29 | 9/23 |
| 复 fù | 82 | 23 | 23 |
| 父 fù | 41 | 19 | 19 |
| 阜 fù③ | 142 | 29 | * |

**G**

| | P | U | UI |
|---|---|---|---|
| 改 gǎi | 51 | 20 | 20 |

---

① Also see radical character (传) zhuàn
② Also see radical form (⺈) dāozìtóu
③ Also see radical form (阝) zuǒěrduō

# Appendix 4  Index of Characters

| | P | U | UI |
|---|---|---|---|
| 感 gǎn | 59 | 21 | 17 |
| 港 gǎng | 19 | 17 | 6 |
| 歌 gē | 91 | 24 | 11 |
| 戈 gē | 71 | 22 | * |
| 格 gé | 152 | 30 | 24 |
| 根 gēn | 153 | 30 | 30 |
| 跟 gēn | 30 | 18 | 7 |
| 挂 guà | 81 | 23 | 23 |
| 轨 guǐ | 49 | 20 | 20 |
| 过 guò | 39 | 19 | 5/22 |

### H

| | P | U | UI |
|---|---|---|---|
| 海 hǎi | 42 | 19 | 17 |
| 行 háng① | 11 | 16 | 6/7/24 |
| 航 háng | 41 | 19 | 19 |
| 号 háo/hào | 29 | 18 | 7/22 |
| 很 hěn | 10 | 16 | 1 |
| 后 hòu | 61 | 21 | 21 |
| 忽 hū | 59 | 21 | 17 |
| 户 hù | 29 | 18 | 23 |
| 沪 hù | 133 | 28 | 28 |
| 花 huā | 112 | 26 | 9 |
| 化 huà | 9 | 16 | 16 |
| 坏 huài | 9/131 | 28 | 28 |
| 欢 huān | 91 | 24 | 2 |
| 环 huán | 123 | 27 | * |
| 悔 huǐ | 59 | 21 | 21 |
| 会 huì | 9 | 16 | 5/27 |
| 或 huò | 71 | 22 | 8 |
| 获 huò | 112 | 26 | 24 |

### J

| | P | U | UI |
|---|---|---|---|
| 集 jí | 21 | 17 | 17 |
| 急 jí | 59 | 21 | 19 |
| 挤 jǐ | 81 | 23 | 20 |
| 季 jì | 91 | 24 | 24 |
| 加 jiā | 40 | 19 | 19 |
| 柬 jiǎn | 152 | 30 | 25 |
| 简 jiǎn | 73 | 22 | 22 |
| 件 jiàn | 10 | 16 | 8/23 |
| 讲 jiǎng | 71 | 22 | 22 |
| 交 jiāo | 154 | 30 | 3 |
| 郊 jiāo | 154 | 30 | * |
| 胶 jiāo | 155 | 30 | * |
| 跤 jiāo | 155 | 30 | * |
| 饺 jiǎo | 141 | 29 | 29 |
| 绞 jiǎo | 155 | 30 | * |
| 较 jiào | 49 | 20 | 13 |
| 校 jiào② | 155 | 30 | 7 |
| 节 jié | 112 | 26 | 19 |
| 结 jié | 101 | 25 | 25 |
| 姐 jiě | 10 | 16 | 5 |
| 巾 jīn | 92 | 24 | 26 |
| 京 jīng | 154 | 30 | 3/27 |
| 睛 jīng | 144 | 29 | * |
| 精 jīng | 145 | 29 | 29 |
| 景 jǐng | 142 | 29 | 24 |
| 静 jìng | 19/145 | 29 | 18 |
| 净 jìng | 19 | 17 | 13 |
| 竞 jìng | 72 | 22 | 22 |
| 酒 jiǔ | 19 | 17 | 14/25 |
| 就 jiù | 73 | 22 | 22 |
| 举 jǔ | 153 | 30 | 25 |
| 剧 jù | 122 | 27 | 27 |
| 绝 jué | 100 | 25 | 21 |
| 均 jūn | 130 | 28 | 17 |

### K

| | P | U | UI |
|---|---|---|---|
| 看 kàn | 61 | 21 | 8 |
| 客 kè | 111 | 26 | 6/23 |
| 肯 kěn | 121 | 27 | 19 |
| 空 kōng/kòng | 20 | 17 | 7/17 |
| 款 kuǎn | 92 | 24 | 21 |

### L

| | P | U | UI |
|---|---|---|---|
| 拉 lā | 82 | 23 | * |

---

① Also see character (行) xíng

② Also see character (校) xiào

| | | | | | | | | |
|---|---|---|---|---|---|---|---|---|
| 郎 láng | 102 | 25 | 25 | | **N** | | | |
| 乐 lè[①] | 123 | 27 | 27 | | P | U | UI | |
| 累 lèi | 49 | 20 | 16 | 哪 nǎ | 29 | 18 | 1 | |
| 里 lǐ | 61 | 21 | * | 那 nà | 101 | 25 | 2/18 | |
| 理 lǐ | 122 | 27 | 27 | 难 nán | 21 | 17 | 15 | |
| 礼 lǐ | 102 | 25 | 25 | 脑 nǎo | 121 | 27 | 27 | |
| 厉 lì | 120 | 27 | 27 | 闹 nào | 100 | 25 | 25 | |
| 历 lì | 120 | 27 | 16 | 内 nèi | 154 | 30 | 23 | |
| 力 lì | 40 | 19 | 21 | 能 néng | 121 | 27 | 21 | |
| 立 lì | 72 | 22 | * | 暖 nuǎn | 141 | 29 | 17 | |
| 利 lì | 122 | 27 | 5/27 | | | | | |
| 连 lián | 39 | 19 | 19 | | **P** | | | |
| 脸 liǎn | 121 | 27 | 18 | | P | U | UI | |
| 炼 liàn | 29 | 18 | 18 | 跑 pǎo | 30 | 18 | 18 | |
| 量 liáng/liàng | 61 | 21 | 21 | 泡 pào | 104 | 25 | * | |
| 零 líng | 21 | 17 | 17 | 炮 pào | 104 | 25 | 29 | |
| 路 lù | 30 | 18 | 3 | 培 péi | 131 | 28 | 22 | |
| 论 lùn | 70 | 22 | 21 | 赔 péi | 132 | 28 | 28 | |
| 旅 lǚ | 92 | 24 | 13/24 | 批 pī | 81 | 23 | 23 | |
| 律 lǜ | 10 | 16 | 16 | 聘 pìn | 71 | 22 | 22 | |
| | | | | 平 píng | 21 | 17 | 17 | |
| | **M** | | | 破 pò | 133 | 28 | 28 | |
| | P | U | UI | | | | | |
| 妈 mā | 133 | 28 | * | | **Q** | | | |
| 马 mǎ | 133 | 28 | 1 | | P | U | UI | |
| 玛 mǎ | 134 | 28 | 1 | 其 qí | 31 | 18 | 18 | |
| 蚂 mǎ | 134 | 28 | * | 气 qì | 20 | 17 | 6/17 | |
| 码 mà | 133 | 28 | 21 | 汽 qì | 19 | 17 | 3 | |
| 骂 mà | 134 | 28 | * | 前 qián | 51 | 20 | 14/20 | |
| 每 měi | 41 | 19 | 7 | 欠 qiàn | 91 | 24 | * | |
| 眠 mián | 61 | 21 | 18 | 亲 qīn | 51 | 20 | 12/20 | |
| 免 miǎn | 60 | 21 | 21 | 轻 qīng | 49 | 20 | 14/20 | |
| 面 miàn | 73 | 22 | 2/22 | 青 qīng | 144 | 29 | * | |
| 民 mín | 93 | 24 | 6/24 | 清 qīng | 144 | 29 | * | |
| 母 mǔ | 41 | 19 | 19 | 蜻 qīng | 145 | 29 | * | |
| 目 mù | 60 | 21 | * | 晴 qíng | 145 | 29 | * | |
| 某 mǒu | 152 | 30 | 22 | 情 qíng | 144 | 29 | 22 | |
| | | | | 请 qǐng | 70 | 22 | 3/23 | |

[①] Also see character（乐）yuè

# Appendix 4  Index of Characters

| | | P | U | UI |
|---|---|---|---|---|
| 秋 | qiū | 90 | 24 | 18 |
| 球 | qiú | 123 | 27 | * |
| 区 | qū | 153 | 30 | 30 |
| 趣 | qù | | | |
| 全 | quán | 9 | 16 | 16 |

## R

| | | P | U | UI |
|---|---|---|---|---|
| 容 | róng | 111 | 26 | 17 |
| 如 | rú | 10 | 16 | 7/18 |
| 入 | rù | 83 | 23 | 23 |

## S

| | | P | U | UI |
|---|---|---|---|---|
| 色 | sè | 60 | 21 | 18 |
| 纱 | shā | 101 | 25 | 25 |
| 山 | shān | 143 | 29 | * |
| 衫 | shān | 113 | 26 | 26 |
| 赏 | shǎng | 132 | 28 | 24 |
| 稍 | shāo | 90 | 24 | 20 |
| 社 | shè | 102 | 25 | 24 |
| 申 | shēn | 83 | 23 | 23 |
| 身 | shēn | 31 | 18 | 18 |
| 圣 | shèng | 131 | 28 | 26 |
| 师 | shī | 92 | 24 | 1/16 |
| 失 | shī | 31 | 18 | 18 |
| 湿 | shī | 20 | 17 | 17 |
| 石 | shí | 132 | 28 | * |
| 实 | shí | 112 | 26 | 26 |
| 始 | shǐ | 10 | 16 | 11 |
| 史 | shǐ | 10 | 16 | 16 |
| 示 | shǐ[①] | 102 | 25 | 26 |
| 视 | shì | 102 | 25 | 9 |
| 试 | shì | 71 | 22 | 8/22 |
| 收 | shōu | 51 | 20 | 22 |
| 首 | shǒu | 31 | 18 | 18 |
| 书 | shū | 103 | 25 | 25 |
| 暑 | shǔ | 142 | 29 | 22 |
| 术 | shù | 152 | 30 | 27 |
| 束 | shù | 152 | 30 | 25 |
| 顺 | shùn | 83 | 23 | 23 |
| 私 | sī | 91 | 24 | 20 |
| 松 | sōng | 152 | 30 | 16 |
| 送 | sòng | 39 | 19 | 16 |
| 诉 | sù | 70 | 22 | 6 |
| 宿 | sù | 111 | 26 | 24 |
| 算 | suàn | 73 | 22 | 8/20 |
| 碎 | suì | 133 | 28 | 26 |
| 岁 | suì | 143 | 29 | 29 |
| 所 | suǒ | 30 | 18 | 16 |

## T

| | | P | U | UI |
|---|---|---|---|---|
| 讨 | tǎo | 70 | 22 | 21 |
| 挑 | tiāo/tiǎo | 81 | 23 | 22 |
| 条 | tiáo | 152 | 30 | 23 |
| 贴 | tiē | 132 | 28 | 25 |
| 挺 | tǐng | 80 | 23 | 16 |
| 通 | tōng | 39 | 19 | 3/22 |
| 投 | tóu | 81 | 23 | 22 |
| 吐 | tǔ/tù | 29 | 18 | * |
| 团 | tuán | 110 | 26 | 24 |
| 推 | tuī | 81 | 23 | 14/21 |
| 退 | tuì | 39 | 19 | 19 |

## W

| | | P | U | UI |
|---|---|---|---|---|
| 外 | wài | 144 | 29 | 9 |
| 完 | wán | 111 | 26 | 12/18 |
| 网 | wǎng | 62 | 21 | 21 |
| 旺 | wàng | 142 | 29 | 24 |
| 忘 | wàng | 59 | 21 | 16 |
| 为 | wéi/wèi | 153 | 30 | 2/19 |
| 围 | wéi | 111 | 26 | 26 |
| 位 | wèi | 19 | 16 | 6 |
| 温 | wēn | 20 | 17 | 17 |
| 稳 | wěn | 91 | 24 | 23 |
| 无 | wú | 62 | 21 | 21 |

---

[①] Also see radical form ( 礻 ) shìzìpáng

175

## X

| | P | U | UI |
|---|---|---|---|
| 夕 xī | 143 | 29 | 29 |
| 吸 xī | 29 | 18 | 22 |
| 息 xī | 60 | 21 | 21 |
| 习 xí | 114 | 26 | 26 |
| 喜 xǐ | 103 | 25 | 2/25 |
| 细 xì | 101 | 25 | 24 |
| 夏 xià | 82 | 23 | 17 |
| 险 xiǎn | 143 | 29 | 28 |
| 线 xiàn | 100 | 25 | 23 |
| 详 xiáng | 93 | 24 | 24 |
| 享 xiǎng | 154 | 30 | 30 |
| 肖 xiāo | 62 | 21 | * |
| 削 xiāo | 62 | 21 | * |
| 宵 xiāo | 62 | 21 | * |
| 消 xiāo | 62 | 21 | 21 |
| 霄 xiāo | 63 | 21 | * |
| 销 xiāo | 60 | 21 | 21 |
| [校] xiào | 155 | 30 | 7 |
| 效 xiào | 50 | 20 | 18 |
| 谢 xiè | 70 | 22 | 5 |
| 欣 xīn | 92 | 24 | 24 |
| 信 xìn | 9 | 16 | 15/23 |
| 型 xíng | 131 | 28 | 21 |
| [行] xíng | 10 | 16 | 6/7/24 |
| 幸 xìng | 103 | 25 | 25 |
| 续 xù | 100 | 25 | 23 |
| 穴 xué | 20 | 17 | * |
| 雪 xuě | 21 | 17 | 17 |
| 旬 xún | 142 | 29 | 24 |
| 训 xùn | 71 | 22 | 22 |

## Y

| | P | U | UI |
|---|---|---|---|
| 沿 yán | 20 | 17 | 17 |
| 眼 yǎn | 61 | 21 | 21 |
| 羊 yáng | 93 | 24 | * |
| 洋 yáng | 93 | 24 | * |
| 氧 yǎng | 93 | 24 | * |
| 痒 yǎng | 93 | 24 | * |
| 样 yàng | 93 | 24 | 7/17 |
| 要 yào | 10 | 16 | 16 |
| 药 yào | 112 | 26 | 18 |
| 页 yè | 82 | 23 | * |
| 业 yè | 62 | 21 | 21 |
| 夜 yè | 144 | 29 | 19 |
| 医 yī | 153 | 30 | 18 |
| 衣 yī① | 113 | 26 | * |
| 易 yì | 141 | 29 | 17 |
| 意 yì | 59 | 21 | 5/17 |
| 邑 yì② | 101 | 25 | * |
| 阴 yīn | 143 | 29 | 29 |
| 音 yīn | 154 | 30 | 30 |
| 饮 yǐn | ... | 29 | 10 |
| 应 yīng/yìng | 40 | 19 | 13/19/22 |
| 营 yíng | 112 | 26 | 21 |
| 用 yòng | 113 | 26 | 26 |
| 由 yóu | 50 | 20 | 20 |
| 又 yòu | 50 | 20 | * |
| 于 yú | 31 | 18 | 18 |
| 雨 yǔ | 20 | 17 | * |
| 玉(王) yù | 122 | 27 | * |
| 预 yù | 82 | 23 | 10/18 |
| 原 yuán | 120 | 27 | 11/19 |
| 院 yuàn | 142 | 29 | 18 |
| 约 yuē | 100 | 25 | 7/20 |
| 越 yuè | 49 | 20 | 20 |
| [乐] yuè | ... | 27 | 27 |
| 运 yùn | 39 | 19 | 18 |

## Z

| | P | U | UI |
|---|---|---|---|
| 再 zài | 154 | 30 | 7/30 |
| 赞 zàn | 132 | 28 | 26 |
| 燥 zào | 29 | 18 | 17 |
| 增 zēng | 131 | 28 | 22 |
| 战 zhàn | 72 | 22 | 22 |

① Also see radical form (衤) yīzìpáng
② Also see radical form (阝) yòuěrduō

# Appendix 4  Index of Characters

| | | | | | | | |
|---|---|---|---|---|---|---|---|
| 站 zhàn | 72 | 22 | 6 | 拄 zhǔ | 11 | 16 | * |
| 招 zhāo | 81 | 23 | 22 | 柱 zhù | 12 | 16 | * |
| 正 zhēng /zhèng | 41 | 19 | 5/17 | 住 zhù | 11 | 16 | 14/24 |
| 征 zhēng | 52 | 20 | * | 注 zhù | 12 | 16 | 17 |
| 怔 zhēng | 51 | 20 | * | 助 zhù | 40 | 19 | 7 |
| 争 zhēng | 73 | 22 | 22 | 祝 zhù | 103 | 25 | 25 |
| 睁 zhēng | 74 | 22 | * | 专 zhuān | 123 | 27 | 27 |
| 筝 zhēng | 74 | 22 | * | 砖 zhuān | 124 | 27 | * |
| 证 zhèng | 51 | 20 | 23 | 转 zhuǎn/zhuàn | 123 | 27 | * |
| 政 zhèng | 52 | 20 | * | [传] zhuàn | 123 | 27 | 29 |
| 症 zhèng | 52 | 20 | * | 隹 zhuī | 21 | 17 | * |
| 挣 zhèng | 74 | 22 | * | 资 zī | 132 | 28 | 22 |
| 支 zhī | 83 | 23 | * | 自 zì | 51 | 20 | 20 |
| 之 zhī | 83 | 23 | * | 总 zǒng | 59 | 21 | 17 |
| 职 zhí | 71 | 22 | 22 | 租 zū | 90 | 24 | 3 |
| 址 zhǐ | 130 | 28 | 20 | 足 zú② | 30 | 18 | * |
| 止 zhǐ | 41 | 19 | * | 族 zú | 92 | 24 | 24 |
| 至 zhì | 31 | 18 | 18 | (阝)zúzìpáng | ... | 18 | * |
| 质 zhì | 132 | 28 | 21 | (阝)zuǒěrduo | ... | 29 | * |
| 舟 zhōu | 41 | 19 | * | (冖)qūzìkuàng | ... | 30 | * |
| 竹 zhú① | 72 | 22 | * | (宀)jīngzìtóu | ... | 30 | * |
| 主 zhǔ | 11 | 16 | 10/22 | | | | |

---

① Also see radical form (⺮) zhúzìtóu
② Also see radical form (⻊) zúzìpáng